Patrick Gilligan Says Be Your Own Boss!

By

Patrick Gilligan

ISBN: 0-75962-848-3

This book is printed on acid free paper.

1stBooks - rev. 5/23/01

"Patrick brings the power of Entrepreneurship down to a see-it, feel-it level… to the realities of doing it!"

- Carleton Sheets
Author of "No Down Payment"
and Host of the longest running infomercial (17 years) on television

"The first 10 years of my career were a struggle. If I would've had a book like this… I would have accomplished some of my goals sooner."

-Ralph Roberts
Best Selling Author of "Walk Like a Giant, Sell Like a Madman"

Dedication

This book is dedicated to the hundreds of Entrepreneurs that I've interviewed and learned from in the business world. My interaction with these intrepid folks is the basis for this book.

A special thanks goes to Linda Nelson Hypio, whose support and encouragement made this book possible.

I also want to thank Carleton Sheets and his marketing company for giving me my first "big break" on National Television.

This book is also dedicated to all Entrepreneurs, those courageous men and women who are the backbone of this great country, and perhaps the world!

TABLE OF CONTENTS

Chapter 1:
INTRODUCTION

<u>THIS BOOK IS FOR YOU IF:</u>

- **You would like to start your own business**
- **You might want to be your own boss in the future**
- **You know someone who wants to be an Entrepreneur**
- **You want to think and act like an Entrepreneur to improve your opportunities at work**
- **And lastly, <u>*Success*</u>—I share a lot of the advice that some of my famous guests shared with me and my audience. Much of that wisdom pertains to success in life as well as Entrepreneurship!**

Welcome to: <u>**Patrick Gilligan Says Be Your Own Boss!**</u> Catchy title. I've been fortunate enough to have been featured in several newspaper and magazine articles, and the Detroit Free Press chose that as the headline of their story on me. You may have seen me and that Detroit Free Press headline and article on the nationally televised Carleton Sheets' program. I've Hosted and been Featured in that program for over two years.

I've had the pleasure of interviewing hundreds of entrepreneurs including some of the most successful people in America: **Paul Harvey, Jack LaLanne, Ed McMahon, Mark McCormack, John Paul DeJoria, Les Brown, Anthony Robbins, Nick Bollettieri, Carleton Sheets, Tom Hopkins, Dick DeVos** and **Brian Tracy.**

I'm also a successful entrepreneur and have reviewed countless books and courses on the subject. I've also given lectures at various universities and other venues.

My book is intended to be a practical, concise, easy to read guide to Entrepreneurship covering all facets of successful business start ups including: Why Become an Entrepreneur, Characteristics of Successful Entrepreneurs, Hot Businesses, Finance, Marketing, Public Relations, Franchises, Real Estate, Multi-Level Marketing Companies, Sole Proprietor vs. Incorporating, the Web, etc. And a special chapter on How to Run a Business from Your Home! **The resource section alone contains over 250 resources:** names, addresses, phone numbers and web sites to aid the entrepreneur.

In short, this is a book written by a Successful Entrepreneur who has interviewed many of the world's best.

Before we get into the heart of the book, let me put you in a positive frame of mind with my signature close from television and radio:

"If you can imagine it, you can achieve it. If you can dream it, you can become it."

As a matter of fact, you'll find positive sayings throughout this book. I believe that a positive mental outlook is essential for success in any aspect of life.

Chapter 2:

WHAT IS AN ENTREPRENEUR?

Let's start by defining the word Entrepreneur. The word comes from the French. My definition is simply that an Entrepreneur is a person who takes on the risks and responsibilities of creating and running a business.

In fact, I believe a true entrepreneur is someone who creates a unique business.

Let me use myself as an example. I have a Bachelor's Degree in Health Services Management and an MBA. Back in the early 80's when I was working on my undergraduate degree, HMO's were just on the horizon. I chose to do my undergraduate internship at an HMO. I wanted to be on the cutting edge of health care.

After college, I worked for a couple of HMO's—a marketing rep for one and a National Account Executive for another. I then secured a position as Director of Marketing for a hospital by the ripe old age of 30!

It was at age 30 that I decided I'd rather call my own shots. So I created a company that specialized in marketing HMO health and dental products to businesses. At the time, some people said, "Who in their right mind would want an HMO plan?" My response was "Let's find out!" At the time, there was only one other company specializing in HMO's. Today, every insurance agent sells them. In less than two years, I developed a client base that paid my bills for years. That's the beauty of selling insurance, <u>residual income</u>—that's a component I look for!

WHY BECOME AN ENTREPRENEUR?

There are a lot of reasons to become an entrepreneur.
- Corporate downsizing/rightsizing, whatever semantics you care to apply. Corporate security just isn't there anymore.
- What about social insecurity? Very few people believe that social security will be able to provide for them when they retire.
- What about attaining wealth? With few exceptions, you'll never get wealthy working for someone else.
- And how about flexibility and lifestyle?

There are a lot of interesting examples of Successful Entrepreneurs. Most successful entrepreneurs start with a vision that satisfies a consumer need. Henry Ford imagined an automobile in front of every home, long before most people thought of owning their own car. Steve Wozniak envisioned a computer in every home at a time when only universities, labs and corporations used them. With his close friend, Steve Jobs, Wozniak founded Apple Computer in his parent's garage in 1975.

During one of my shows I asked the great motivational speaker **Brian Tracy** for his definition of success. He said "Freedom." I think that says it all. Only Entrepreneurs can dictate when and where they will work. Many studies on happiness list a sense of control over ones life (Freedom) as a key to happiness.

With the advances in Technology-i.e. faxes, computers, cellular phones, the Internet—it's becoming easier than ever to become your own boss. In fact, more and more people are starting businesses from home. (By the way, I recommend if it's at all possible to start your business from your home.) Whether you realize it or not, you're living in one of the most exciting times of our country's history, a period that will prove to be the turning point for the livelihood and fortunes of millions of Americans.

Some studies suggest that up to 37 million people—one third of the entire U.S. population—are conducting full or part-time businesses out of their homes, representing a 20-fold increase over the last 10 years. What's more, others predict that by the year 2002, roughly 90 million people in the United States or one out of three will have made the decision to be their own boss, work from the comfort of their homes, and pursue their dreams!

DOES IT PAY TO BECOME AN ENTREPRENEUR?

Research shows that the average employee makes an annual salary of $26,000 while the average home-based business household earns $50,250 a year. Of those home-based business households, 20% earn over $75,000 per year and 66% are owned by women.

Would you like to be a Millionaire? Become an Entrepreneur! Studies show that two-thirds of America's millionaires are self-employed. By the way, most millionaire entrepreneurs did not inherit great wealth. About 80% are first-generation affluent. They just went out and did it—**so can you!**

WHAT CHARACTERISTICS DO SUCCESSFUL ENTREPRENEURS SHARE?

What is a successful entrepreneur? Here are a few interesting tidbits.

- 2/3's of entrepreneurs had at least one parent that was self-employed.
- 60% of entrepreneurs are the oldest child in their family.
- The most successful entrepreneurs have exceptionally supportive spouses. A supportive mate provides the love and stability to balance the insecurity and stress of entrepreneurship. Indeed, even bankers and venture capitalists look very closely at the martial status of the business owner.
- The average age of an entrepreneur is 28.7. There are exceptions however. I've interviewed successful entrepreneurs that were 15 and some that were 65!
- The most common educational level for an entrepreneur—a Bachelors degree.
- Entrepreneurs don't like working for anyone else but themselves. Usually money is a by-product of an entrepreneur's motivation rather than the motivation itself.
- Contrary to popular belief, entrepreneurs are not high-risk takers. They tend to set realistic and achievable goals. And when they do take risks, they're usually calculated ones.
- Organization is the key to business success. Some owners keep lists on their desks, always crossing things off the top and adding items to the bottom. Others use computers, note cards, etc. Systems vary, but you'll never find an owner without one.
- Entrepreneurs are participants, not observers. They're players, not fans.

To be an Entrepreneur is to be an optimist—to believe that with the right amount of time and money you can do anything!

Before we go any further, let's examine the pro's and con's of being an entrepreneur.

<u>PRO'S</u>
1. You are your own boss.
2. You set your own hours.
3. You are in a sense in control of your destiny! Many psychologists believe that <u>control</u> is one of the keys to <u>happiness</u>.

4. There are <u>tax benefits</u>. To the extent they are used for business, you can write off your car, lunches, vacations, house and even your kids. For more information, consult Chapter 14.

<u>CON'S</u>
1. No regular paycheck at the beginning.
2. No benefits—medical, dental, life, pension.
3. Unless you incorporate, you're paying a lot more in taxes.

Chapter 3:

SHOULD YOU BECOME AN ENTREPRENEUR?

Here are a few questions prospective Entrepreneurs should ask themselves:

<u>Are you a self-starter</u>? Do you have the initiative to do more than you are asked to do? Are you resourceful and able to seize opportunity when you encounter it and turn it into your advantage? Employees are used to getting a job and being handed assignments. Entrepreneurs create opportunities—often opportunities that never existed before—and assign themselves tasks.

<u>Are you jumping in headfirst</u>? It's exciting to leap in headfirst into a new business venture. Some people need that shot of adrenaline to get motivated. However, you should build yourself a comfort level at the beginning. Assess your risk-reward ratio, and look for ways to reduce your risk. How do you do that? Perhaps start your venture on a part-time basis.

<u>Do you have a positive, friendly interest in others</u>? If you do, that can be a tremendous asset, especially in a business that requires a lot of face-to-face contact. If you don't—don't fret. There are businesses, for example Mail Order, that don't require great interpersonal skills.

<u>Are you a leader</u>? If you are going to have employees working for you, being a good leader is a must. How do you know? If you're the type of person that people listen to and inspire loyalty—you know! Even companies with full-time Human Resource personnel sometimes find it difficult to hire the best people for a job. Training and retraining people can be a time consuming process. A leader who can motivate and reward employees will get his or her business off to the best start!

<u>Can you handle responsibility</u>? Do you enjoy taking charge? Are you the one who volunteers for tasks or responsibilities at meetings or do you sit quietly while others raise their hands? If you don't you probably won't be a successful entrepreneur.

<u>Are you prepared for long hours</u>? Many people believe that when they work for themselves, they will be working less than they used to. Wrong! Most entrepreneurs find themselves working longer, an average 52.5 hours/week vs. 43.5 hours/week for the typical paid employee.

Now, don't panic. There are a couple of things to consider. When I started my HMO consulting business, I only worked a couple of hours a day. But remember I had a few years of experience in the field, it was a relatively new product, and I was very confident. However, my example is the exception. Also if you have a passion for what you are doing, the hours will fly by and it won't seem like work. A wise person once said that if you love what you do, you'll never work another day in your life!

<u>Are you a decisive thinker</u>? Or are you hesitant, even fearful, about a decision you must make? Are your decisions quick but accurate? The ability to sum up a situation quickly and make realistic choices for action is paramount to being an effective entrepreneur.

<u>Can people rely on you</u>? This is critical. Can people trust you? Do you have integrity? Is your word your bond? A good reputation brings in new clients and helps retain old ones.

<u>Can you stand up to set backs and not quit</u>? Believe me, there will be set backs, even in the most thought out businesses. Can you analyze a problem and take steps to correct it, or will you panic and throw in the towel at the first opportunity? Most people in business are not geniuses, but they have a strong belief in themselves and their ability to succeed.

The most successful multi-millionaires and billionaires that I've interviewed had their share of fights, struggles, battles, setbacks, obstacles, defeats and disappointments. The difference between winners and losers is that losers let these hurdles defeat them. Winners, on the other hand, pick themselves up, learn what they can, and persevere!

One of my favorite interviews was with the great motivational speaker **Les Brown**. He said, "It's not over until I win." And another of his great sayings is "What's next?" In other words, when you encounter one obstacle, go onto the next.

Bill Gates, billionaire owner of Microsoft, said "I'd say persistence is very important. We were totally committed from the beginning. And everything we've done has taken many years. People have doubts when it looks like the business is not going to take off. Business has ups and downs, but so what? We're persistent because we believe in what we're doing, not because of the financial results. Financial results can send short-term signals that can confuse you."

Indeed, another couple of famous entrepreneurs that I've interviewed, **Mark Victor Hansen** and **Jack Canfield**, talk about how publisher after publisher after publisher rejected their now famous best selling book series *Chicken Soup for the Soul.*

And let's not forget **Colonel Sanders** or **Orville Redenbacher**. Colonel Sanders at the age of 65 peddled his now famous chicken recipe to numerous restaurants before he found one, which would try it. Orville Redenbacher had tried and failed for years with his popcorn until one day someone suggested that he put his picture on the package. It made all the difference.

I could spend hours discussing all the successful people I know that overcame adversity and obstacles, but I think you get the point!

<u>Can you adapt to changing situations</u>? To be successful in business, you have to be able to recognize and react to changes in your market, in your customers' preferences, and your competitors.

<u>Do you look for ways to improve efficiency</u>? By constantly looking for ways to improve, many business owners actually find new product/service ideas to improve their business or to start another!

If you answered YES to the aforementioned questions, you probably have what it takes to be a Successful Entrepreneur.

Now, I know that some of you reading this book would like a definitive test to take to know if you have what it takes to be a successful entrepreneur. I've seen dozens of these Entrepreneur tests and quizzes. For those of you that feel you need such a test, I've included one for you. All set—here we go! There's twelve questions that require a YES or NO response.

<table>
<tr><td>1.</td><td>Is it unacceptable for you to be paid below what you are really worth?</td></tr>
<tr><td>2.</td><td>Are you interested in a part-time business to replace/compliment your current income?</td></tr>
<tr><td>3.</td><td>Are you willing to sacrifice your personal time to build long term financial freedom?</td></tr>
<tr><td>4.</td><td>Can you generally make good decisions based on sound information?</td></tr>
<tr><td>5.</td><td>Do people consider you to be honest and a person of integrity?</td></tr>
<tr><td>6.</td><td>Do people (generally) seriously consider what you have to say?</td></tr>
<tr><td>7.</td><td>Do you consider yourself coachable by others?</td></tr>
</table>

8. Are you the type of person who can go the distance in the pursuit of your long-term objectives?
9. When things go wrong, do you accept the responsibility or do you blame others?
10. Will you work hard for something you really believe in?
11. Do you enjoy sharing what you believe in with others?
12. Would you like to take greater control of how you live your life?

Remember, you are to answer *yes* or *no* to these questions. Go back and check your answers. They may surprise you. If you answered YES to 10 or more of the 12 questions—you're on your way to Entrepreneurial Success. If you answered YES to 6-9 questions, you have your work cut out for you. If you answered YES to 5 or less then you may want to consider staying in the corporate world.

If you feel you have what it takes to be an Entrepreneur—let's proceed!

Chapter 4:

WHAT ARE THE HOT BUSINESSES TO GO INTO? IS ONE OF THEM RIGHT FOR YOU?

Now that you've decided to be an Entrepreneur, what business should you get into? There are a number of possibilities. What are the Hot Businesses now?

Entrepreneur Magazine frequently reports on new business and popular trends. Some of their hot business listings include:

Advertising Agency	**Carpet cleaning service**
Audio Bookstore	**Cellular phone service**
Baby store	**Consulting business**
Bed & Breakfast	**Dating service**
Bookkeeping service	**Desktop publishing**
Car wash	**Automobile detailing**

And how about….

Employment agency	**Interior design**
Executive recruiting service	**Janitorial service**
Gift basket service	**Mail order business**
Home inspection service	**Mobile DJ, multi-level marketing**
Image consulting	**Newsletter publishing**
Import/Export	**Self improvement seminars**

And the list goes on and on!

What's right for you? Well if you've ever heard my show or read any of my press, you'd know my answer is: **whatever your particular skills and abilities lend themselves to!** There are no magic, get-rich fields. It all comes down to what your particular skills lend themselves to.

You need to take inventory of your skills. Let's use me as an example. I have an aptitude for Sales, Marketing and Public Relations. Many people have said that I could "sell ice to Eskimos." By the way, the ability to sell yourself is critical to entrepreneurial success! On the other hand, I can work a calculator but I'm not a great numbers person. I wouldn't be any good at running an accounting firm. Some people have said that I'm a great communicator. I enjoy talking to and learning from others. I've been very good at promoting myself. In a four-year time frame, I've been written up some 70 times in the newspapers and magazines, I've gotten myself booked on various talk shows as an expert on Entrepreneurship, and I positioned myself to be selected for national television! A number of people have asked me to represent them as their PR firm.

One of the main ingredients necessary for entrepreneurial success is confidence! One day I woke up and decided I wanted to start my own business—and I did. Then I decided I wanted my own TV show, and then a radio show, and then another business. I truly believe in myself and my abilities. Is that arrogant? Probably. Is it necessary? Definitely!

Larry King was kind enough to call me. Larry called me because, among other things, I sent him a long fax in which I told him that I thought I was one of the best Interviewers in the country! "Really, I'm that good" I said in the fax. "How do I get to your level?" I told Larry that I never went to broadcasting school. He said, "Pat, either did I. If you're good, you're good!"

I had also interviewed the founder of a prominent broadcasting school and I told him that I had an ego. He said, "Pat, if you didn't, you shouldn't be in the business."

Now do you have to be as bold as I am to succeed—NO. But you better have a steadfast belief in yourself or nobody else will!

If you feel you lack certain skills or abilities, find someone who has them. A business associate of mine wanted to start a Human Resource Company. However he wasn't an expert in HR, so he teamed up with a lady who was and in a short period of time they launched and grew a very successful Employee Leasing Company!

I've said it before but it's worth repeating: One of my often-quoted pearls of wisdom is: you definitely have to have a passion for what you want to do. It's been said that if you do what you love to do—you'll never work another day in your life! That's so true.

George Burns once said:
"Do you love what you're doing for a living? That's what's important! It's the secret to long life…to be able to get up in the morning and do something you love to do. And I love what I'm doing. I don't care what you do for a living. Let's say you make felt hats. The only thing that's important is that you make sure you love to make felt hats." Wise man that George Burns!

How do you figure out what you have a passion for or what business you would like? Here's an idea. Review the thousands of businesses listed in the yellow pages or Entrepreneur Magazine. Make a list of the businesses that appeal to you. Then review and dwindle that list down to ten, to five, and ultimately down to one.

What about your natural talents? Simple—make a list of all of your talents. Maybe you're good with numbers, or you're good with people. Some people are good at games like Chess, Scrabble, etc. No matter how insignificant, write it down. You'll amaze yourself.

One enterprising young fellow would go up to the door of the country's first supermarket with a little red wagon and offer to take home groceries for a small tip. He said he was in the transportation end of the food business. His name: **Lee Iaccoca**.

By the way, an ancillary benefit to compiling that list is when you get depressed, you can always trot out the list and give yourself an ego boost.

You should also have an income goal in mind for your new business. Everyone wants to be a millionaire, but how much do you really need per year for the next five years. Remember, income potential of businesses differ. A small home-style restaurant will be hard pressed to earn a six-figure profit, yet a fast food franchise may.

And what about Image? Do you care about status (it does matter to most of us, even though we say it doesn't.)? You'll want to choose a business that fits your ego. Example: would you open a portable toilet business, even though it could be very profitable?

Another of my often-quoted tips is to get 2-3 years experience working for someone else. If you recall, I worked for a couple of different HMO's before I started my own consulting business. That experience was invaluable. Not only did I learn a lot about the industry, but I made a lot of great contacts, and most importantly, I developed confidence in my ability to successfully market managed care programs!

Chapter 5:

ARE MULTI-LEVEL MARKETING COMPANIES, MAIL ORDER, REAL ESTATE AND FRANCHISES FOR YOU? WHAT ABOUT BUYING AN EXISTING BUSINESS?

All right. Let's turn our attention to the numerous types of business ventures you could get involved in. Let's begin with:

MULTI-LEVEL MARKETING COMPANIES

Multi-Level Marketing Companies are also known as MLM's. I interviewed the President of probably the granddaddy of all MLM's, Amway, and I've looked at many of them including NuSkin, Mary Kay, Excel, and Prepaid Legal. MLM's have been around since the 1950's. You've probably been approached by one or more of these companies yourself.

The basic idea behind MLM's is simple: as an independent contractor, you buy products from an MLM at wholesale prices and resell them at a 35-50% markup. You can really make money when you recruit 5 other people, and they recruit 5 other people, until by the 6th level you have over 1,000 in your group (referred to as a <u>downline</u>.) Then you make a commission each time someone in your downline sells something.

Here's the Pro's and Con's of MLM's:

<u>**PRO'S**</u>
1. MLM's are one of the few opportunities where you have the potential to make a lot of money (some folks claim to make over $10,000 a month) with a nominal risk. Typical cash outlay is a few hundred to a few thousand dollars.
2. You also earn residual income in MLM's which is great.
3. You can work from your home.

<u>**CON'S**</u>
1. Over 25,000 companies have attempted to establish a presence through MLM. Only a handful have succeeded. Why? At some point the majority of these companies become unwieldy. The market for their product becomes saturated, competition from similar

organizations squeezes them out, new recruits become disillusioned, and the structure begins to topple.

2. The pressure to join one of these companies can be tremendous. The promise of instant wealth, of belonging to a special group of super achievers, of being part of a revolutionary new organization can be compelling!

Here's my best advice on MLM's:

- You need to be almost a "Cheer Leader" to make money; you must motivate people to sell and stick with the plan. You'll have to be patient, energetic, extroverted and enthusiastic to succeed.

- Work with solid well established companies that have been around for over two years. However, I believe you would have less opportunity to amass great wealth with a company like Amway because it has been around so long and there are a lot of people ahead of you.

- You want a company that has a tangible product to sell. If you like a company and think it will last, perhaps others will too.

- The best products have a high profit margin (retail price is five times the manufacturing cost) and are consumable (vitamins, cosmetic creams, etc.).

- Ask the person recruiting you what level they're on. You must be reasonably close to the top of any subgroup within the company to earn the top commissions.

- Make sure the company you are thinking of joining is operating legally. There is a legal distinction between certain kinds of pyramid schemes and true MLM companies. Contact your local Better Business Bureau or State Attorney General's Office before making any commitment.

REAL ESTATE

A lot of people in this country earn extra income by owning real estate. How do you make money in R/E? One way is to rent out properties i.e.: single family houses, apartments, etc. Another is to "flip" property—that is buy and then sell a piece of property at a substantial profit!

I know we've all seen infomercials on television hawking real estate and a host of other products. Are they for real? Well, I looked into several. As you know, I am appearing on the Carleton Sheets' National TV Infomercial. Of all I reviewed, I found his to be the best. His course was comprehensive and easy to understand. And I spoke to several of his students who actually used the principles taught in his course.

Can you really buy property with <u>no money down</u>? The answer is <u>yes</u>. If you are going to try real estate, I'd recommend Carleton's course.

Other thoughts on real estate—<u>learn</u> all you can. Take a couple of courses, read books, etc. The reality is you need to be good with people. You'll be doing a lot of negotiating with owners, bankers and tenants. You'll have to go out and look at a lot of properties before you locate those gems. The main idea taught in a lot of these courses is that you are looking for flexible owners—people that need to sell soon i.e.: being transferred, divorced, etc.

If you are a good negotiator and you can get comfortable with being a landlord, there are some definite benefits to being a Real Estate Investor.
1. Build a nice residual income from your rental properties. And remember—your properties can't ever fire you or cut you out of a deal!
2. There are still some nice tax benefits to real estate ownership, not to mention the appreciation gains each year. Many R/E investors actually zero out their taxes because of their properties!

EXISTING BUSINESS

How about buying an existing business? According to the SBA, 80% of people that go into business for themselves don't give much thought to buying an existing business or franchise, yet both offer significant advantages.

The success rate is much higher for those who buy an existing business than that of first time entrepreneurs. About 3 million businesses change hands each year. That means 8,000 businesses are sold every day! Businesses with a net worth of $100,000 or less change hands every 4 years on average.

The <u>advantages</u> of buying an existing business:
1. <u>Immediate cash flow</u>. A successful business will return a profit much faster than a new business. Many new businesses don't bring in enough money during the first year to pay the owner a reasonable salary—if at all.
2. <u>Clientele</u>. An existing business already has an established clientele. Usually most have established good relationships with bankers, suppliers and customers.
3. <u>Employees</u>. You get experienced employees.
4. <u>Owners experience</u>. You can usually enlist the previous owner's aid. They can help establish good relationships with existing customers and suppliers. They can advise you on the quirks of the business and help

you avoid making costly mistakes. However, be prepared to offer some compensation for the previous owners continuing participation in the business!

Some <u>disadvantages</u> of buying a business:
1. <u>Bad lease</u>. Maybe the rent is too high or the landlord is unwilling to transfer from the previous owner. My advice—determine how long the lease has to go and see if it's exchangeable. If it's for a brief time, renegotiate before the business is purchased.
2. <u>Bad will</u>. Perhaps the previous owner hadn't done such a great job with his business.
3. <u>Facilities in disrepair</u>. Perhaps the facility has been poorly maintained.
4. <u>Bad inventory</u>. Perhaps the inventory is damaged or outdated. My advice—Check the inventory and make sure it is appropriately priced.
5. <u>You paid too much for the business</u>. If you overpay, your profit will be limited. My advice—get a qualified business appraiser to determine a solid price!

One question you should definitely ask yourself is <u>why are they selling</u>? Bad health, divorce, burnout, retirement—these situations could create a great opportunity for you. You may be able to buy it well below the market cost.

Where do you find businesses for sale? Newspapers, Business Brokers, Bankers, Attorneys, Accountants and Trade Associations are all excellent sources. And just like real estate, it's possible to buy a business with no money down. How? People like Ted Turner get rich acquiring businesses through <u>leveraged buyouts</u> (that is using the assets and cash flow of the business to finance the entire purchase price.) You can use the same principles. There are many strategies available to you. I'll discuss one here.

This strategy involves the use of factors. You find a business with good sales, but unable to expand due to slow collections and the amount it has tied up in accounts receivable. Then you engage a Factor, who will buy your accounts receivable at a discount, and can wait 30 to 60 days for payment. By the way, I happen to own a Factoring Company. If I can be of service in this regard, call me at (248) 258-7760.

In summary, buy the business by factoring the A/R and use the proceeds for the <u>down payment</u>. Then factor new receivables as fast as they come in to obtain additional working capital.

Another option: SBA and Banks. Visit the SBA or Bank Liquidation officers. They may have dozens of loans that have gone bad and almost all of these loans are for sale.

FRANCHISES

Let's examine buying a franchise. It's pretty obvious that franchises are everywhere these days. And more are on the way. A new franchise opens somewhere in America <u>every 8 minutes</u>! There are over 1,000 firms with close to a million units that account for about 1/3 of all retail sales, almost $500 billion.

Exactly what is a franchise? The International Franchise Association defines a franchise as "a continuing relationship between the <u>Franchisor</u> (Business) and the <u>Frachisee</u> (You) in which the Franchisors knowledge, image, success, manufacturing, and marketing techniques are supplied to the Franchisee for consideration."

Buying a franchise may be more attractive than starting a business from scratch. Lack of seasoned business experience often makes entrepreneurs uneasy about going it alone. A lot of people want to open a business but they lack a specific idea, product, service or location.

Before we look at the pro's and con's of franchises, let's examine what's in it for the people that sell franchises (Franchisors). Money—a lot of Money! Specifically, franchise fees, capital acquisition and reduced marketing.

<u>PRO'S OF OWNING A FRANCHISE</u>
1. <u>Instant recognition</u>. People are more aware of McDonalds than Joe's Hamburgers. The day you open a McDonalds you have instant customers.
2. <u>Promotion</u>. Even if Joe's Hamburgers were 100 times better than McDonalds, you'd have to spend a fortune on advertising before you'd attract customers.
3. <u>Cookie cutter/Cookbook approach</u>. The Franchisor will provide you with an extensive training manual that covers just about everything from training, advertising, employment and processing. I'd bet that most new business failures would have paid handsomely for such a "Business Bible." Most of the guesswork is gone—they provide you with all the answers.
4. Probably the greatest advantage is that the <u>failure rate is much lower</u> with franchises, about 1/16th that of small independent businesses. Why?
   - Typically it is easier to obtain funds from banks and investors.

- Usually it produces a profit sooner than the typical new business.

CON'S OF OWNING A FRANCHISE
1. You must follow their program to the letter! A franchise works best when people follow a proven system. There's an inherent conflict right there. I see entrepreneurs as risk takers, not order takers. Many people come to realize that they are too headstrong for a franchise relationship.
2. You will have little to say over product and marketing strategy.
3. It is very expensive to start—5% of the gross sales for continued support.
4. They may not be flexible when you want to sell.

Who is today's Successful Franchisee? Entrepreneur Magazine says today's average Franchisee is 40 years old; has a net worth of $330,000; 90% are college graduates; 2% are women; 11% are minorities.

If you are seriously considering a franchise, my advice is to conduct your own independent market research and take a close look at the location. Use an Independent Financial and Legal Consultant to assess the potential worth of the business and to prevent contractual conflicts with the Franchisor.
- A Franchise lawyer can charge between $100-$150 an hour.
- Get a list of every Franchisee. Select about 10 and call them.

Franchisors are required to give you a Uniform Franchise Offering Circular referred to as a UFOC at least 10 business days prior to signing a contract with you. Take a close look at it. It contains 23 items of information and runs as much as 100 pages. It provides a revealing glimpse of the Franchisors financial status and operating procedures.

Probably the best thing you can do is to work for someone in that field or even for that franchise. Wendy's founder **Dave Thomas** worked for Colonel Sanders for years before he founded his own franchise.

Where do you locate a Franchise? Entrepreneur Magazine has franchise opportunities plastered all over their pages. Also USA Today, Wall Street Journal and any number of books provide them.

If you want the security of a franchise and are willing to pay for it, then it may be a good option for you. However, I don't consider people that own franchises to be True Entrepreneurs. But then, what do I know?

How much money can you make? Fortunately franchise regulations prohibit Franchisors from making unfounded claims of profitability, and they strictly regulate almost all the information that Franchisors provide. <u>My best advice</u>: ask existing franchise owners about their financial performance. Many will be uncomfortable discussing it with you, but some will tell you. If you find a receptive franchise owner, you may want to follow him around for a few days— nothing beats first hand knowledge. Take plenty of notes. The more questions you ask, the more likely the franchise owner will be to open up to you.

MAIL ORDER BUSINESS

What about a mail order business? The biggest advantage of course is that you can remain anonymous. The biggest single factor in mail order is finding the right product, ideally one that has universal appeal and solves a problem. Example—everyone is into fitness these days, especially the aging Baby Boomers. The ideal product, "Abs of steel in 30 seconds a day" solves a problem and solves it quick! You want a product that has a high mark up, at least 4 to 1. If a product costs you $1, you want to be able to sell it for $4.

Many companies will drop ship your products for you (they will send it directly to your customers) so you don't need to maintain an inventory.

How do you find the right product? There are literally hundreds of companies that produce products you can sell. Go to your local library and do some research.

By the way, does your product have to be some revolutionary new product to be successful? NO! As a matter of fact, some companies are strictly copycats. They look for products that are successful and make a minor adjustment to it, then market the products themselves.

When you find that great product that people can't live without, then you place ads in newspapers, magazines, the Internet, or create your own catalog. Don't forget to investigate the smaller papers. Sometimes they have great rates.

The most important part of your ad is the headline. It has to grab attention. Make them short and attention grabbing. There are a variety of books on how to write great headlines. There's no rejection in mail order. Remember, nobody is going to read your ad and call you up and say they don't want your product!

WHEN IS THE BEST TIME TO START A BUSINESS?

If you are an unfortunate victim of corporate downsizing—turn that misfortune into your own good fortune. Start your own business! You've undoubtedly picked up a great deal of knowledge and business savvy in those years in Corporate America. You probably received some type of severance package, or at the very least, you can collect unemployment. Take all that experience (and money) and start that business you've always dreamed of!

Another good time to start a business—how about during a recession? Why? Key business resources are cheaper, so you get started for less money. Examples:
- Real Estate is cheaper. Landlords, anxious to unload some of their commercial space may offer you free rent for up to a year.
- Easier to get employees. More people are unemployed and are typically willing to work for less.
- There are bargains in capital equipment. Suppliers are hungrier and are apt to be more flexible and aggressive in their pricing and credit terms.
- During tough times Customers are more willing to try new products and services.

Companies best able to take advantage of a recession are:
- <u>Labor intensive</u>-cheaper labor
- <u>Cash based</u>—business that takes payments in cash as opposed to waiting on struggling companies to pay their bills is in a great position.
- <u>Capital generating</u>—business that can generate capital internally from earnings and not have to rely on banks is on solid ground.
- <u>Capital equipment intensive</u>—this business has an advantage. Business liquidations abound making everything available (desks, computers, copiers, etc.) at great savings.

If you can develop products or services that are cutting costs or adding value, you're going to be in high demand. The bottom line here is if you have the cash, a recession may be a great time to start a business.

Chapter 6:

WEALTH BEGINS AT HOME—A MINI COURSE IN STARTING AND RUNNING A HOME-BASED BUSINESS

TEN MYTHS ABOUT HOME-BASED BUSINESSES

1. Working from your home is preferable to working at an office.

    Actually, this is <u>TRUE</u>. Working from home gives you the greatest flexibility and freedom. Believe me, if you've worked from your home for a while—you won't want to go back.

2. You have to be a great salesperson to be successful.

    Actually, this is partially true. Some experts will argue that there are a number of businesses (i.e. Income-Tax preparer, Accountant, etc.) that can prosper without you being a good salesperson. I disagree. You have to get the word out about your business to make money, and that involves sales. The good news is that even if you're not a naturally gifted salesperson, most of the hundreds of entrepreneurs that I've interviewed over the years—have a real passion for what they are doing. Passion and enthusiasm sells!

3. You can't make any money working from home.

    That's a bunch of ____! I personally know several people who work primarily from their home and make six figures. Will you make a lot of money from your home? If you find a niche, go about it smartly, and finish reading this book—you stand a pretty good chance.

4. You can't work with kids at home.

    One of the benefits of working from home is that it gives you the opportunity to be closer to your family. This can be accomplished by setting a regular business schedule and communicating it to your family, have your kids watched by someone else (i.e. grandparents, babysitters) and set a policy that you are not to be disturbed during business hours, unless it is an emergency.

5. If you're at home, you're not working.

    I remember when I first starting working from my home, my mother would call me and ask me to take her somewhere. When I'd say I couldn't, she would say, "Why, what are you doing?" I'd respond by saying "Mom, I'm working. How do you think I pay for my house, car, etc.?" (By the way, sometimes she still asks me that question, and I've worked out of my home for over a decade.)

6. It doesn't take much money to start a business from your home.

    This is partially true. While many home-based businesses can cost thousands to launch, many can be started for a few hundred. I started my first home-based business some 12 years ago for about $100.

7. If you work from home, you don't have a real business.

    Nothing could be further from the truth! Just ask the home-based entrepreneurs who make six figures a year if their businesses are real.

8. You can work in your underwear if you want to.

    Actually this is partially true, although I wouldn't recommend it. When I'm making phone calls for business, I'm usually dressed casually, i.e. sweatpants, T-shirt, etc. Being comfortable is another great benefit of being a home-based entrepreneur. Even Corporate America is catching on with their casual days, typically Fridays.

9. You can write everything off.

    Not true. However, you can write off just about all of your expenses as they relate to your home business: office supplies, travel, postage, utilities, etc. Check with your tax expert. By the way, you can write that off too as business tax return preparation.

10. You can't go back.

    Why would you want to? But, if circumstances are such that you have to go back to the corporate world—I submit you are in a very strong position. Look at all the experience and success you've had. Today's corporate employees need to think like entrepreneurs anyway. It's just a matter of selling yourself!

THERE'S NO PLACE LIKE HOME FOR RUNNING A BUSINESS

As I mentioned earlier in the book, I'd highly recommend working from your home if at all possible. I know a little about running a business from home—I've worked out of my home for over a decade. Of course, I host my radio and television programs from radio and television studios. Although, I know hosts who do their shows from studios in their homes. I may consider that as an option for the future.

There are a lot of advantages to working out of your home:
- No commute to and from work.
  I tell people I have a 30-second commute to my home office.
- You control the environment.
  You set the thermostat, music, etc.
- Tax benefits.
  You can write off the portion of your home that you use exclusively for business.

Some of the advantages of running your business from home can be a mixed blessing. As a home-based entrepreneur, you can set your own schedule. Many times there will be a tendency to sleep in, watch television, or a whole host of other distractions.

Here's a suggestion.
Tell people around you, friends, family, neighbors, etc. that working out of your house means just that—working out of your house. From 9-5 (or longer) you are at work.

Even still, that television or sleeping in can seem pretty inviting. Here are some things I do.

Most of the work that I do involves making phone calls and sending out faxes. Ideally, you should be up and ready to go no later than 9 a.m. Since there's no commute, you can probably get up at 8:30 and be ready by 9:00. However, when business is slow and you really don't feel like making those calls, give yourself a break.

On occasion, I'll sleep in late—maybe even blow off the whole morning, and work out, play tennis, watch TV, etc. Then my conscience kicks in. "OK, you've blown the morning, you've had a good time. Now, let's get to work." So I'll hunker down and make phone calls non-stop for the remainder of the day.

As for TV, working out, etc. view these activities as rewards for a job well done. If I put in a good day on the phone, I'll give myself the luxury of knocking off at 4 p.m. so I can beat the rush at the gym.

Set goals and objectives for every day. Get yourself a good business calendar. I use Day-Timers. I like the Day-Timer format because it gives you two pagers per day. The left page has things to be done (action list) and the right page has times 7 a.m.—9 p.m. for appointments. There's also an area to record your expenses. If you looked at my personal Day-Timer, you'd see a list of things to be done each day. As I accomplish each task, I check it off.

People always ask me how I'm able to handle everything on my plate, i.e. my TV, radio, consulting businesses, etc. It's simple. I make a list of things that need to be done each day, in order of their importance. If I don't get to each item on that day's list, I move it to the next day's list.

When I started my HMO consulting business out of my home, I had to generate clients. So I bought some business directories and started making calls. Typically I'd make 10 new contacts a day, and follow up on contacts from the previous day. I did this Monday through Friday morning. I took Friday afternoon off.

I didn't have a lot of money when I started, so I had to be creative. I sold a lot of dental insurance through one particular managed care plan. After a day on the phone, I'd call the dental company and have them mail out a customized proposal along with a letter from the President of the company that included my company name, phone number, etc. Not only did this technique save me a lot in postage, it also saved me the time it would have taken to mail out that information.

I employed another technique to save time, money, and wear and tear on my car: I hooked up with a Rep from a large local life insurance company, who had use of a company car. He sold primarily a product called payroll deduction Universal Life. Employers could offer this plan to their employees and have the employees pay for it though a payroll deduction. Remember, I was selling Managed Care Health and Dental Care products to employers. So I'd set up several appointments a week. The life insurance Rep would pick me up at my house and take me to the appointments. After I'd made my Health and Dental pitches, the Rep would do a presentation on the Universal Life product. If they wanted the life policies, I got a commission on it—which I received for over a decade. As it turned out, I rarely drove my car on appointments the first couple of years of my business. Besides the cost savings, I enjoyed having someone in my industry to talk with.

YOUR HOME-BASED BUSINESS OFFICE

Let's talk about setting up your Home Office. What exactly are you going go need?

✓ **The Office itself**

Ideally, your office should be used solely for business. Probably the most common location for a home office is a spare bedroom or den. You definitely want a room with a window so that you can look outside on occasion.

✓ **Telephones**

You'll want to install a separate business phone line for your home office. If you're going to have a computer, you'll need a phone line for it. (I hate it when I call someone and their line is busy because they've hooked up their computer to their one line.)

✓ **Hands-Free Headset**

If you're going to be making a lot of phone calls at a stretch, you should definitely consider a headset for your telephone. You'll find that when you've made a lot of calls, you'll get tired of holding the phone handset. Another option is to use the speakerphone (provided your phone has one), although many speakerphones have limited distance microphones. You'll get tired of sitting and talking in one position. With a headset, you can stand and walk around the room while you are talking.

You can get a headset at a store like Radio Shack. The headset costs about $20 as does the headset control module that it plugs into. You may need to buy an adapter. They run about $5.

✓ **Wireless Phones**

Cellular phones and digital phones are ubiquitous these days. They can be fairly inexpensive, even cheaper than using a regular phone. If you conduct a lot of business away from your office, this may be a viable option for you. Be especially careful when using one of these devices while driving.

✓ **Fax Machines**

I couldn't operate without my fax machine. It's inexpensive and immediate. My fax machine is an all-in-one phone/fax/copier/answering machine. I paid less than $200 for it. It saves me time, money and space by taking on the functions of many other office machines. I'd highly recommend it over a standalone fax that simply receives and sends faxes. You can also use your computer as a fax; however, your computer has to be on for it to work.

✓ **Copiers**

As I just mentioned, an all-in-one fax/copier can be used to make copies. For a few hundred dollars, you can buy a small desktop copier from warehouse stores and office supply superstores.

✓ **Computers**

Most home-based Entrepreneurs have a computer these days. If you decide to get one, there are several options:

- <u>Desktops</u>: Desktop computers are probably the most common used in home offices. They have the most powerful microprocessors (which make them fast), the most memory, the largest monitors, and the latest technology (like faster modems for connecting to the Internet.) Prices vary, but expect to pay about $1,000 for a basic model and between $2,000 and $3,000 for a top-of-the line model.
- <u>Notebooks</u>: A notebook is essentially a miniature desktop (also known as laptops.) If you're on the road a lot, this may be a good option for you. Expect to pay around $1,000.
- <u>Palmtops</u>: Also referred to as Personal Digital Assistants (PDA's), they are primarily used to track appointments, phone numbers and to-do lists.
- <u>Printer and Scanner</u>: If you get a computer, you'll want to get a printer as well. To print letters, invoices, proposals, flyers—you'll need a printer. At present, there are two types of printers. You may want to consider laser printers (black, white and color text) and color ink-jet printers for graphics and photos. You may want a scanner to input photos and graphics. You'd be amazed at what you can do with an ink-jet printer!

Note to the wise: Computers are always getting faster and cheaper. Do your homework and shop them!

- ✓ **Internet Access**
  If you're going to get a computer and a printer, you may as well go on line! If you don't have Internet access in today's world, you're out of it. It is literally a gateway to the world! America Online, AT&T and Microsoft Network (MSN) all offer inexpensive packages. With Internet access, not only will you be able to email your friends and family, but also your clients and prospective clients!
- ✓ **More Office Equipment Basics**
  - <u>Desk</u>: Get a good one. The **BIGGER** the better. You'll want room for your telephone, computer monitor and keyboard, and enough space to spread out your work.
  - <u>Chair</u>: Same advice. Get a good one. You're going to be spending a lot of time in it, so make it comfortable as well.
  - <u>File Cabinets</u>: You'll need file cabinets to house your files and paperwork.

- <u>Storage</u>: Closets, garages, attics are all great places to store paperwork, brochures and other work related items. *A little known fact: You can write off storage space on your taxes if you take the Home-Office deduction.* (Check with your CPA or tax specialist.)

✓ **Tons of Office Supplies**

The Office Supply Superstores have the best selections and typically the best prices. Stock up during sales. (Some business associations offer a discount on office supplies.)

✓ **Lighting**

Make sure your home office is well lit. Not only will you be able to see what you're doing more clearly, but good lighting keeps your spirits up, especially on a cold, dreary day!

Don't drain your savings building a great Home Office. Here are **15-1/2** cost savings ideas.

1. **Shop Office Supply Superstores.**

   As I mentioned earlier, you can get great deals at Office Max, Office Depot, Staples, etc. I bought my file cabinets at Kmart for less than $10.

2. **Check out Office Liquidation sales.**

   You can pick up office furniture at these sites for pennies on the dollar. Check your local newspapers for dates and time.

3. **Build your own Furniture or unassembled Furniture.**

   If you're handy and have the time, you can save a lot of money.

4. **Estate Sales.**

   Not only can you pick up some inexpensive items for your home, but you may find some gems for your home office. For local sales, check your newspapers, or drive around the neighborhood and look for Estate Sale signs.

5. **Manufacturers Outlets.**

   You may have to drive a little ways, but there may be some great bargains awaiting you. Heck, make a day of it!

6. **Floor Models.**

   Display units are almost always sold at a discount. While they'll probably have a little wear and tear, they are generally covered under full warranty. Try and negotiate the best price you can.

7. **Business Liquidation Sales.**

   A close cousin to Estate Sales. Businesses go out of business every day. (Their owners probably did not read this book!) Check your local classified ads.

8. **Private parties.**

   Again, check your classifieds and want ads for individuals looking to sell their furniture.

9. **Sales and Rebates.**

    This is kind of obvious. If you can, wait until the item you want is on sale or has a rebate.

10. **The Internet.**

    You can find some great deals on just about anything on the Internet.

11. **Auctions**

    A close relative of Estate Sales and Business Liquidation Sales. Don't forget to check out on line auctions such as eBay. Again, check out the classifieds in your local paper.

12. **Ask for a business discount.**

    It never hurts to ask!

13. **Business Charge Cards.**

    I'm inundated with business charge cards. Not only do they have generous limits, but they allow you to separate your business and personal spending. And companies like Hertz, Mobil, FedEx will give you discounts when you use their card.

14. **Compare Telephone Rates.**

    The deregulation of the telecommunications industry can mean savings and freedom for you. You can choose your provider of long distance calls, in-state calls, wireless and Internet connections. Do your homework.

15. **Join an Association.**

    As I mentioned earlier, many professional and trade associations offer discounts on a variety of products and services: office supplies, health insurance, travel, etc. Also, association fees are typically tax deductible and associations offer a great way to network.

½   **Recycle your Fax Paper.**

    If you use a plain paper fax like I do—take the unwanted faxes you receive, flip them over and reuse them to send out or receive future faxes.

FINANCE FOR THE HOME BASED ENTREPRENEUR

Although Finance is discussed in greater detail in Chapter 8, let's take a look at some specifics for those of you that work out of your home (or plan to). Let's keep the cash flow flowing! Here are a few ideas to keep the cash coming in.

<u>If at all possible, get your money up front.</u>

I handle the advertising and collections for my radio program. I remember telling my CPA years ago that I was planning to start my own radio show. He told me that he had a client that had his own radio program and was owed over $40,000 for ads. So from day one I billed my radio clients, and I don't play their commercials until I've received their payment first. (The exception: I've billed a few clients who ran their ads over several months.) Has the policy worked for me? Some 4 years and 50 advertisers later, I've received every penny, and only had one late payment! And they were in arrears for only 6 weeks. Remember, nothing beats cash!

<u>Timely and accurate invoices.</u>

Send out invoices as soon as you deliver a production service, preferably with the delivery itself. To help prevent delayed payments, make those invoices accurate.

<u>Pay your bills as late as you can.</u>

I always pay my bills within about 3 days before they are due. This is a good policy for both personal and business bills.

<u>Bill your clients monthly.</u>

As opposed to quarterly. The more often you bill your clients, the more often you'll get paid (within reason.)

<u>Give discounts for prompt payments.</u>

This will encourage your clients to pay on time. A lot of Real Estate investors who rent out properties use this technique. For example, rent on a particular property is \$550 due by the 5th of each month. If paid by the 1st, it is only \$500. (Of course, if you're a savvy investor, the \$500 payment is still profitable for you.)

<u>Paste little stickers on your invoices.</u>

A little sticker on an invoice gently reminding your client of the date it is due, can go a long way toward a prompt payment.

> *"In my factory we make cosmetics, but in my stores we sell hope."*
> **-Charles Revson**, Founder of Revlon Cosmetics, Inc.

Chapter 7:

EVERYTHING YOU ALWAYS WANTED TO KNOW (NEED TO KNOW) ABOUT MARKETING, PUBLIC RELATIONS, ADVERTISING AND SALES. HOW TO BECOME AN EXPERT IN YOUR FIELD.

MARKETING

MARKET YOUR BUSINESS FOR SUCCESS

Let's take a look at probably the most important avenue to business success: MARKETING. What is Marketing? Marketing is simply the means by which you communicate to your market the products or services that you offer. This encompasses Sales, Advertising and Public Relations. Many people think Marketing and Sales are the same thing. As I just pointed out, Sales is part of Marketing—a very big part! Although I do understand the confusion. During my first few sales jobs, my business cards said Marketing Representative on them. Indeed, even when I was a Marketing Director, most of my time was spent selling.

Any marketing class you may take dating back to the Stone Age includes the four "P's of Marketing."

1. <u>Product</u>   The product (or service) should meet a customer need.
2. <u>Price</u>   The product has to be priced low enough for the public to buy it and high enough for the business to be profitable.
3. <u>Place</u>   The product should be sold where there is a demand for it and where customers can easily find it.
4. <u>Promotion</u>   Advertising and Public Relations.

Ideally, you want your product or service to fill a niche in a given market. Be a visionary, look to the future. As previously mentioned, back in the early 80's, I found a niche in the health care field. I believed managed care was the future of health care and I was right (for better or for worse.) So I created a company that directly marketed managed care plans to local corporations. I secured contracts with most of the local HMO's that would pay me an ongoing commission for new business I brought them.

HOW DO YOU FIND A NICHE?

"If you want to succeed, you should strike out on new paths rather than travel the worn paths of accepted success."
--John D. Rockefeller

Market research is a good place to start. Your proposed company should solve a problem or offer some demonstrably better service, product or price than the existing competitors.

A practical approach to market research is to identify or capitalize on a given niche in a marketplace. Take these steps:

1. Identify a market you would like to compete in. For example, let's say you wanted to create your own HMO. Ideally you or your partner would have worked for an HMO or been a member of one.
2. You would contact all the HMO's in your area and review their brochures and see what they are offering.
3. Contact HMO customers in your area to determine their level of satisfaction with a given HMO.
   a) What is the HMO doing right?
   b) What is the HMO doing wrong?
   c) What changes would you like to see in their service, benefits, pricing?
4. Construct your own model of the perfect HMO. Include the best elements of the HMO's you reviewed and eliminate or lessen the worst aspects.

This formula works extremely well! I've interviewed several entrepreneurs who have used this model or variations of it, to establish successful businesses.

There are a lot of names for niche marketing. Target marketing and concentrated marketing are probably the most common. There is a downside to niche marketing. Suppose you manufacture only one type of designer hats for women. If that style goes out of style—you may be out of business.

You also have to constantly monitor your market for change. A few years after I was almost exclusively selling managed care programs in Metro Detroit, the other million or so insurance agents in the area also started marketing HMO plans. Then came the insidious "Agent of Record" letter offered by most insurance companies. With this letter, companies could simply name another agent to handle their account and you were out in the cold. I lost a lot of accounts and over a hundred thousand dollars in commissions because of agents who handled other lines of insurance for the client would say, "Why don't you let me handle your health insurance too—just sign this Agent of Record letter." Over time, the niche I had carved out for myself in the Health Care Field eventually cost me.

My strategy to counter the dreaded letter was to start working with PEO's (Professional Employer Organizations). PEO's outsource the Human Resource functions of a company, handling payroll, employee benefits, tax fillings, etc. Just like the HMO's had, PEO's pay me an ongoing commission for bringing them clients. The only way I can lose the business is IF:

A. The client goes out of business
B. The client goes with another PEO
C. The client decides to drop the PEO services

All are real possibilities. There is no perfect scenario!
What can you learn from my experience?

1. Stay on top of the market. Watch it closely.
2. Have a Plan B. My Plan B was the PEO's.
3. Diversify. Offer alternative products outside of your niche. If I would have had other insurance lines, I might have kept some of the clients I lost.

Although, I really like the concept of PEO's. By handling a lot of a company's administrative burdens, they allow the client to get back to their core business. And PEO's have saved many of my clients money in the process.

That's another key in Marketing and Sales! You should feel good about what you are marketing. Your product or service should definitely benefit your customers!

<u>WHAT SHOULD YOU KNOW ABOUT MARKET ANALYSIS?</u>

Let's talk about Market Analysis. Is opportunity really knocking or are you setting yourself up to be knocked out? Remember, the way to make money is to satisfy someone else's needs. Market analysis is not a perfect science, it is the study of people and their constantly changing likes and dislikes. However an accurate market analysis can save you a lot of money and time!

Why do most businesses fail? Because there just isn't any need for the product or service. Before I started my health care consulting business, I worked for a couple of HMO's and I knew that Health Care was a commodity that everyone needed. And I knew that HMO's offered more benefits for less money than traditional insurers.

Here are some practical ways to conduct a market analysis:
1. Start with your own ideas, experience and knowledge. Just as I had knowledge and experience in health care, you have experience and knowledge in your field.
2. Talk with professional associates, friends, family, etc.
3. Look at the players in the field. Examine their marketing materials. Talk with them. Determine what they do well and what they don't do well. Then create your own model.

There are a number of publications that contain information for your market research and give it free to potential advertisers. Loan officers at local banks who handle small business accounts may have some helpful information for you. Some Universities have Small Business Institutes that serve small businesses. Chambers of Commerce and Trade Associations may also have useful information.

Surveys can also be instructive and effective. When I was working for an HMO, they were planning to expand their network to a new territory. I called on companies in this new territory and said we were planning to move into the area. I asked if they had a few minutes to participate in a market survey. A few months later, I called them back and let them know that the network was up and running. I already had detailed information on them and it was not a cold call because I had spoken with them before.

<u>MARKETING PLANS</u>

You really should have a Marketing Plan. A marketing plan is simply a written summary of all the great ideas you have for promoting your business. It outlines all of your marketing goals and strategies, along with the actual methods you will use to achieve them. Your marketing plan should also include timelines and deadlines for achieving your goals.

A marketing plan can be as simple or as complicated as you want. If you're a one-man band, perhaps it need only be one page. You can expand it as your business grows.   Some corporate marketing plans are practically as big as phonebooks. Your marketing plan should:

1. Identify your target market and future customers (including applicable demographics, i.e. age, income, gender, etc. and trends [economical, technical, and social] that may affect your customers).
2. Distinguish the unique advantages of your product or service from your competitors.
3. Identify and probe the strengths and weaknesses of your competitors, including their market shares.
4. Indicate where to focus your marketing efforts.
5. Position your product or service for maximum sales.
6. Identify the most effective sales and advertising strategies.
7. Schedule for the implementation of each marketing phase.
8. Projections of the revenues you plan to generate and the anticipated sales needed to achieve your revenue/profit goals.
9. Overall budget for marketing, sales, promotions.
10. Pricing strategy. Determine a price for your product or service that will allow you to cover your costs, be competitive in the marketplace and still make a profit.

If your Marketing Plan answers these questions sufficiently—it could double nicely for a Business Plan.

GREAT WAYS TO MARKET YOUR PRODUCTS OR SERVICES

Give speeches and hit the rubber chicken circuit by making yourself available to speak to every professional, fraternal and service organization in town. The Lions, Rotary, Kiwanis, Optimists and the Chambers are always looking for speakers.

Join networking groups. It will cost you some money and you may have to get up awful early, but you will meet a lot of people and hopefully get some referrals. Don't expect to have people give you leads right away. It may take several weeks before people feel comfortable enough to give you leads. Remember, you have to give to get. Also you may want to consider getting involved in the leadership of your organization or chapter. Many times they may even waive or reduce your dues!

Speaking of <u>referrals</u>—word of mouth advertising is probably the best there is. It's free and can be very powerful! Think about it. If a friend of yours recommends a particular restaurant, movie or lawn service, you're probably more inclined to try it. A referral is in effect an endorsement of you or your product, or both. How do you get referrals?
Ask for them! Of course, it's best to ask for a referral after you have had a client for a while and have done a great job for them. Take a moment to thank those that send you referrals. Send a thank you note (handwritten on a note pad). If it turns out to be a big client—buy them a gift or take them to lunch.

<u>It's better to give than receive.</u> When you are in a networking situation and you come across someone who you think can refer business to you—ask them how you can help them. It puts you in a very good light and makes them more receptive in wanting to reciprocate the gesture.

OTHER MARKETING IDEAS:

> - **<u>Press Releases</u>**: Always contact the media when your company does something noteworthy. Press releases can cover new products, new clients, awards, special events, anniversaries, new staff, promotions, etc.
> - **<u>Articles</u>**: Getting published in the magazines and newspapers your customers read is an excellent way to establish yourself as an expert in your industry. In the first two years I was on radio, I garnered over 40 stories on myself. That's millions of people who've read about me. Also consider writing a column. You probably won't get paid but it's great exposure!
> - **<u>Newsletters</u>**: Another effective Marketing tool is newsletters. Ever popular, newsletters are an efficient way to communicate with your market. Studies indicate that people are much more likely to read a newsletter than any other piece of direct mail advertising. Keep them short, informative and entertaining.
> - **<u>Seminars</u>**: Consider offering a seminar. Almost any business has the potential to offer seminars in a professional, sales or technical capacity. A computer store might hold a half-day free session on how to maintain a computer and avoid service calls. A building supply could offer a series of classes for do-it-yourselfers.
> - **<u>Charities</u>**: Get involved in charities. It may be a little expensive, but you'll meet the who's who of your town.

> **Giveaways**: Everybody loves to get something for free! They don't have to be expensive, but they should be useful. I think coffee mugs with your company name and logo can be extremely effective. There's almost a subliminal effect at work here. If a decision-maker is drinking his/her coffee everyday out of your mug, you are that much more recognizable when you call on them.

> **Volunteering**: There are a lot of community-based organizations that would love to put your special talents to work for them: animal shelters, homeless shelters, churches, soup kitchens, etc. Volunteering is a great way to meet people who you may someday do business with. Besides, you're helping your community and those less fortunate!

> **Sponsorships**: Consider sponsoring a local kid's football team, soccer team, parade, etc. It may cost more, but it's probably better to be one of the major sponsors for a given event because your name will be more prominent and you won't get lost in a sea of sponsors.

> **The Web** is also a great way to market your products. (See Chapter 12)

PUBLIC RELATIONS

I love PR. I handle all of the PR for my Radio and TV shows. I started doing my own PR out of necessity. I couldn't afford to hire a big, prestigious firm to handle my PR so I did it myself. I'm glad I did because I learned I was a natural at it. I've had other companies try to hire me to handle their PR. In the last four years, I've been written up in over 75 newspaper and magazine articles, gotten booked on numerous radio and TV shows, and positioned myself to be put on National Television.

You never know if you'll be good at something until you try it.

Exactly what is Public Relations and how does it differ from Advertising? It's simple. PR is Free. Advertising you Pay for!

Public Relations is the dissemination of information (typically through Press Releases) to the general public to favorably enhance the reputation of you, your product and service. Did I mention that PR is free? A good PR firm will charge you upwards of $100 per hour. The target for all of your PR efforts is all of the Media (print and electronic). That's potentially millions of people.

Always contact the media when you or your company does something noteworthy. Press Releases can cover new products, new clients, awards, special events, anniversaries, new staff, promotions, etc.

ADVERTISING

HOW DO YOU GET FREE ADVERTISING? BECOME AN EXPERT.

How do you do that?

<u>Write a Book.</u>
Most people think that someone who has written a book must be an expert on the topic of the book. And they probably are. I can tell you from personal experience that by the time you've finished all of your research and actually written a book of any consequence—you will be an expert, even if you weren't one when you started! After you've written the book, alert the Media.

<u>Host your own TV or Radio Show</u>
There are plenty of cable TV systems throughout the country. Most of these systems have something called "Public Access." Through local Public Access you can take classes on television and production, then create and host your own show. Public Access is free and the participants are volunteers, so be nice to them. I got my start in Public Access. I hosted an award winning show called "Entrepreneur Spotlight." Then I took the show to the radio airwaves. Speaking of <u>Radio</u>, you can approach radio stations in your area and pitch an idea for a show. If they don't bite and you still want to host your own radio show, then approach a brokered station. Most areas have Brokered Stations, which allow you to purchase the airtime yourself. Radio airtime, although much less expensive than television, can get pretty expensive. If you go the brokered route, be prepared to spend some time and effort—securing sponsors to cover your costs.

Hosting your own show can be a lot of fun. It's a great way to meet people and do some networking at the same time. I've turned some of my guests into business clients.

As I mentioned, television time is very expensive. However, if you have the money or sponsors, you can purchase TV time. Frankly, a lot of shows on radio and television are brokered in some fashion.

TO ADVERTISE OR NOT TO ADVERTISE?

As I mentioned, the best form of advertising is free (Public Relations). Do you have to advertise to be successful? NO. But it helps.

I built a successful consulting business without advertising, as have many others. However, if you have the budget for it, almost all types of businesses can benefit from some form of advertising. Advertising is simply a way to get the word out about your company, products or services. You pay for advertising, whereas PR is free.

In addition to calling attention to your company, I think advertising (if done well) brings a certain credibility to you. If you can afford to advertise, you must be a player of some standing.

TYPES OF ADVERTISING

There are various forms of advertising: Newspapers, Television, Radio, Yellow Pages, Directory Listings, Magazines, Internet, Billboards, Direct Mail and Transit. Let's take a look at each.

NEWSPAPERS
Newspapers are an inexpensive way to advertise. They have a lot of advantages.
- <u>Cheap</u> (relatively), your cost per person reached is nominal. Typically, papers with larger circulations will charge more than smaller papers with fewer readers.
- <u>Flexible</u>, you can place or change an ad on relatively short notice. You can design your ad anyway you want and place it practically anywhere within the paper. Speaking of ads, most people like to look at ads, even when they aren't planning to purchase the advertised items.
- <u>Easy to track</u>, you can use coupons to track which paper your patrons saw your ads in.
- <u>Large audience</u>, some newspapers reach millions of readers.

Tips on purchasing newspaper space:
You know which papers are prominent in your local area. Which ones do you read and which ones do your customers read? Which newspapers do your competitors routinely advertise in? Always ask for discounts on multiple ads.

TELEVISION
Television is probably the most expensive medium to advertise in and perhaps the most effective. Seeing is Believing! Everyone watches TV to some degree. There are some definite advantages to television.
- <u>Huge audience</u>, like newspapers, the reach of television is incredible. Almost 100% of homes in any given area have at least one TV set.

- <u>Effect,</u> because television has both an audio and visual effect, it can impact people in a way no other medium can. Think of the most memorable commercials that you've witnessed in your lifetime. You probably saw them on television.

Tips on buying television time:

Although time on television is expensive, the proliferation of all these cable channels increases opportunities for affordable spots. You can purchase commercial spots on TV in increments of 10, 30 or 60 seconds. I've personally starred in both 30 and 60-second commercials. 30-second spots are the most common, because 10-second spots are too brief and typically 60-second commercials are too expensive.

Costs are a function of message length, broadcast time and frequency, and the popularity of particular shows. Popularity is measured in GRP's (Gross Rating Points), one GRP equals 1% of all homes with TV sets in a given area. Example, a show with a rating of "10" is reaching 10% of homes in that market.

A share is the percentage of TV sets in operation that are tuned in to a particular program. Example, a program broadcast at 2 a.m. might have a rating of "2" but a share of "43." Translation—2% of all TV homes, but 43% of all the sets that are on at one time.

Negotiate for lower rates, more slots and better times.

Television time is negotiable. Obviously, prime time is the most expensive. After 11:00 p.m. and early morning slots are typically the cheapest. The airwaves are filled with commercials at the wee hours of the morning. Think of all the infomercials you've seen at these times. The ads must be effective, because they keep showing them.

<u>RADIO</u>

If you can't afford television ads, radio is probably the next best thing. Like television, radio advertising is sold in 10, 30 and 60-second blocks. 60-second spots are the most common and effective. As with television, you can also sponsor sporting events, newscasts, etc.

A unique aspect of radio is that you have a captive audience. Typically, you listen to radio in your car. There are fewer stations on radio than there are channels on television.

Probably the cheapest way to buy radio advertising is on a "run-of-the station" basis meaning the station can drop them in whenever they choose, rather than in fixed time slots. The most expensive time slots are morning and evening rush hours referred to as "drive time" 6 a.m.—10 a.m. and 3 p.m.—7 p.m. Midnight to 5 a.m. is the cheapest.

Radio Advertising Tips:

What stations do you listen to? How about your customers? The business and news stations are usually a good bet, but don't forget the oldies and sports stations. Check a station's Arbitron ratings (Arbitron is the most well known service that rates radio stations on their listenership.) Keep in mind that radio stations pay a fee to be rated by Arbitron and that some of your smaller stations can't afford to be rated. Another question—what stations, either AM or FM, do your competitors advertise on?

YELLOW PAGES AND OTHER DIRECTORIES

Yellow Pages are the place to be if you're a lawyer, plumber, towing service, lawn service, etc. Many times when someone goes to the Yellow Pages, they are ready to buy now. You can also be creative with your ads in the Yellow Pages, using pictures, graphics, etc.

Yellow Page ads can be very effective and very expensive. Decide if the traffic generated by placing these ads will justify the cost.

There are a variety of other directories that you may want to consider: professional, industry, trade association, etc. If you choose one of these, make sure your future customers are likely to see your advertisement. Although many directories are published yearly, many have a shelf life of much longer. If you can't afford a big ad in the Yellow Pages, consider an enhanced directory listing. Instead of the standard one liner, spend a few more bucks to buy and opt for boldface type.

MAGAZINES

There are magazines these days for just about every business and hobby you can think of. Magazines offer some advantages over other types of media:

- Visual Impact, especially on those magazines with a heavy paper stock. Some of the higher-end magazines look like a work of art.
- Focused Magazines usually target specific audiences.
- Shelf Life. Magazines usually have a longer shelf life than other periodicals.

- Verifiable Circulation. Typically, magazines have their circulation audited yearly by an independent agency. The exceptions are regional and special interest publications.
- Regional Packages. Many national magazines permit you to run an ad in some of their market areas only, for less than half the cost of a national ad.

Considerations for buying ad space in magazines:
1. Expensive. Advertising in magazines is a lot more expensive than advertising in newspapers. A 1-½ inch classified ad can cost over $1,000 for one insertion in a national magazine. The Los Angeles Times with a daily circulation of over one million, charges less than $200 per inch for advertisers in it's weekday editions.
2. Lead-Time. You may have to submit your ad as much as two months in advance.
3. Flexibility. Magazines are not as flexible as newspapers. Depending on the publication, you'll be required to buy an ad 1/2 1/3, 1/4 or 1/6 of the page.
4. Internet and the Web. Check out Chapter 12 for advertising statistics on the Web.

BILLBOARDS

Outdoor advertising has its advantages:
1. Inexpensive. They are economical in terms of what you pay for them and their cost per thousand viewers.
2. Exposure. Billboards are seen repeatedly because people usually go the same way to and from work, etc.

But they also have a few limitations:
1. In passing: You pass by billboards quickly. They don't have a lot of time to catch and hold your attention.
2. Display time: Generally to be effective, these signs must be up for at least several weeks.

Other considerations:
- A standard billboard, measuring 12 feet by 25 feet, is sold by "showings" (traffic count). For example, a 100 showing means that 100% of the audience in the market area saw your billboard.
- Prices vary, depending on the market you're in and traffic routes. In one market of 20,000 a 100 showing for five non-illuminated billboards costs about $700 monthly. Rates are generally discounted if you maintain a minimum showing over a given period of time.

DIRECT MAIL

We all hate to get junk mail (known as Direct Mail by those that send it to you.) However, when properly planned and targeted it can be a cost-effective way of getting your message in front of your potential customers. There are many forms of Direct Mail; fliers, brochures, postcards, letters, coupons, inserts and circulars. Direct Mail is best for soliciting phone calls, orders, sales call follow up, sales, etc.

There are pro's and con's to Direct Mail:

PROS

- Quick Feedback. You should know within a few days if your mailing was effective.
- Attention Getter. If only for a few seconds, it should get the attention of your prospect.
- Focused Marketing. Providing you use a good mailing list, you should be able to target exactly the prospects you want.

CONS

- Bad Lists. If you purchase bad mailing lists (outdated or incorrect information) it will be ineffective and a waste of money.
- Low Response. A 2% response rate is typical.

How do you conduct a direct mail campaign? Probably the easiest way is to use existing lists culled from customer receipts, charge accounts slips, redeemed coupons, etc. You can also purchase mailing lists from mailing houses, list brokers, magazines, government bureaus, etc. These are compiled by various criteria such as income, age, zip code, etc. Mailing lists can run from $50 to several hundred dollars.

TRANSIT ADVERTISING

We've all seen them—ads on the sides of buses, taxis, subway cars, just about anything that moves. The biggest advantage is exposure. The biggest disadvantage is cost. You could spend thousands a month in a Metropolitan area on bus advertising.

Harvey MacKay, in his book *Swim with the Sharks without Being Eaten Alive* had a clever twist on transit advertising. He put ads on the top of trucks. His rationale was that a lot of people work in high rise office buildings and are frequently looking down. Good Idea.

WHICH MEDIA SHOULD YOU USE?

As you have read, there are a lot to choose from. You have to answer a few questions.

1. Which Media (TV, radio, newspapers,etc.) best serves what you are selling?
    If you're selling diamond jewelry for instance, television may be your best medium because seeing the jewelry is probably very effective.
2. What is your Budget?
    Your budget will probably dictate which media to use. Perhaps start with local newspapers, and as your company grows, graduate to radio and television.

Advertising on the Cheap.
Co-op advertising is a great way to stretch your advertising dollar. Basically, co-op advertising is sharing the cost with manufacturers, distributors or retailers under certain conditions. Newspaper co-op deals are the most common. How can you get in on a co-op deal? Contact companies offering co-op advertising.

A few words on Advertising Agencies. If you have a limited budget, consider being your own agency. With a little homework and research, you can contact local media and if so inclined, place your own commercials and save the commissions that would otherwise go to the agency.

Which ads really work? According to a survey by DiMassimo Brand Advertising, these ads were among the most effective in 2000.

Top 5 Most Talked About Ads
1. Budweiser: *Whazzzzup!*
2. Snickers: *Voting Booth*
3. Geico: *Collect Call*
4. Jeep: *Jeep Dog*
5. Gap: *Musicals*

Top 5 Ads that Made People Laugh
1. Budweiser: *Whazzzzup!*
2. UPS: *Fulfillment issues*
3. TiVo Launch: *Montana/Lott Masculine Itch*
4. Jeep: *Jeep Dog*
5. Corn Flakes: *Corn Inspection*

Top 5 Ads that People Found Themselves Singing and Humming
1. Gap: *Musicals!*
2. eToys: *Facing Future*
3. Volkswagon: *Da Da Da*
4. Old Navy: *Item of the Week*
5. Priceline.com: *William Shatner's Improvs*

Top 5 Ads that Drove People to Log-on to the Internet
1. E*Trade: *Out the Wazoo!*
2. Kozmo.com: *Cheating Heart* (**tied**) Amazon.com: *Holidays*
3. eToys: *Construction*
4. SmartMoney.com: *Crisis of Confidence*
5. Monster.com: *Get Me Ted*

Top 5 Ads that Drove People to Use a New Service
1. UPS: *Fulfillment Issues!*
2. EDS: *Cat Herders*
3. Geico: *Collect Call*
4. FedEx: *Croc Hunter Snake Bite*
5. TiVo Launch: *Montana/Lott Masculine Itch*

Top 5 Advertising Icons
1. Red: *M&Ms!*
2. Sockpuppet: *Pets.com*
3. Bunny: *Crunch Fitness*
4. Political cartoons: *Snickers*
5. Simon: *MySimon.com*

Top 5 Ads that Had Nothing to do with the Product
1. 7-Up: *Make 7-Up Yours!*
2. Gap: *Musicals*
3. Corn Flakes: *Corn Inspection*
4. TiVo Launch: *Montana/Lott Masculine Itch*
5. Budweiser: *Wasabi*

Top 5 Ads that People Remembered Most
1. Budweiser: *Whazzzzup!*
2. UPS: *Fulfillment Issues*
3. Jeep: *Jeep Dog*
4. TiVo Launch: *Montana/Lott Masculine Itch*
5. Discover: *Danger Kitty*

> *"Everyone lives by selling something."*
> **--Robert Louis Stevenson**

SELL, SELL, SELL

Sales make the world go round. You can have the greatest product in the world, but it has to be sold by someone to someone.

Make everyone your sales person! This is the biggest advice I can give any burgeoning entrepreneur. Multi-level marketing companies have successfully used this technique for years. They know that everyone knows several people.

Let's take it a step further. From the beginning, establish a simple compensation plan that will pay individuals a referral fee for leads that turn into sales. They can be a one-time fee or an ongoing commission. By all means—put it in writing. It's one thing to say, "I'll pay you a hundred dollars for every referral that turns into a sale," and quite another to put it in writing. Try to single out people who have a lot of contacts. But don't exclude anyone—you never know who might bring you a deal!

I once read about a guy who "birddogs" for real estate investors. He has agreements with them that if he finds them good investment properties, he receives a finder's fee. So on weekends, he gets in his car and drives around neighborhoods for a few hours, jotting down addresses of promising properties. I read that he makes over $50,000 a year driving around neighborhoods on weekends!

Target groups that could refer business to you. For instance, if you have a tax product or payroll service, contact CPA's. Call on them individually or arrange group presentations.

Entrepreneurs are sales people. Over 40% of people that start their own business have a sales or marketing background. As I've said before, passion sells. Most of the dozens of entrepreneurs I've interviewed have had a real passion for their business.

In fact, I believe we are all in sales. We're selling ourselves, an idea, etc. By the very nature of being in business for oneself, you've had to sell a variety of people:

- Family Members on this crazy scheme you have of starting your own business.
- Banker on the viability of your business.
- Employees, if you have them, you had to convince them to leave their previous job to follow your dream.
- First Few Customers, you had to get them to believe in you and your company.
- Yourself (probably the toughest of all.)

I believe sales has 7 keys which are:
1. Likability
   People buy from people they like.
2. Integrity
   To be a successful salesperson, entrepreneur, or anything else, you better have integrity.
3. Understanding your Customers
   Your customers are **KING**. Treat them that way. Without them, you'd be out of business. Get to know them and their needs.
4. Know Your Product or Service
   Become an expert, not only on your product or service but also on your competitor's. Why? So you can diplomatically point out how your company has an advantage over your competition.
5. The Art of Persuasion
   Be persistent, professional and nice. Be a consultant as opposed to a salesperson.
6. Dress the Part
   It almost goes without saying that you should dress neatly, wear nice suits, keep hair trimmed and shoes shined, etc. Don't be afraid to dress down for a client. If you are calling on an auto repair shop, don't wear a three-piece suit.
7. Never Be Late
   Always be on time or a few minutes early. When you're late for an appointment, you're in effect saying, "Your time isn't valuable to me." Think like the legendary football coach **Vince Lombardi**, "If you're on time—you're late."

Let's talk a little more about **integrity**. I recently interviewed one of America's top Financial Experts, **Tom Hakim** on my radio show. When I asked him for his advice on success, he said in part, "Integrity ranks first, second and third." I totally agree.

Many years ago when I first started my HMO consulting company, I represented an HMO that prided itself on offering a total coverage plan. No co-pays, no deductibles—full coverage. I sold one of these total plans to a local company. A few weeks later, I got a frantic call from my contact person at that company. Apparently one of their employees required a hearing aid. They were told that hearing aids were not covered under their health plan. I immediately called that HMO. I was told that they had changed their coverage. I guess I didn't get that memo. The HMO plan refused to back me. As I mentioned, I was just starting out at this time and I didn't carry liability insurance. Some of my colleagues in the industry advised me to walk away from my client. After all, it was a small group. My commission on that client was nominal. And, I was told that the client probably would not sue me. There was one problem. I had told this client that hearing aids were covered. Of course, to my knowledge this was true. The HMO had left me twisting in the wind. Here's what I did. I told my client that I would pay for the hearing aid out of my own pocket. I asked them the have the employee who needed the hearing aid to get a few different prices. I took the middle quote. I think I paid $700 out of my pocket for that hearing aid. Believe me, that was a lot of money when I was first starting out. But I felt good—because I did the right thing!

Did my integrity pay off? No and yes. Even though I had paid for the hearing aid out of my own pocket, the client told the HMO that they did not want me as their agent. So even though I had done the right thing, I was going to lose my measly commission and I was out the $700 for the hearing aid. Shortly after, I received a letter from my managing agent (a go-between hired by the HMO to work with agents, administer commissions, etc.) The letter indicated that they had heard about me paying for the hearing aid and that they were impressed with my integrity. Furthermore, they took it upon themselves to pay me the commissions on that group. Over the years, I received approximately 4X more in commissions on that group then I paid for the hearing aid. Integrity is key!

Of the various ways to get sales appointments, I think telemarketing is among the most effective. In fact, I built my consulting business primarily by making cold calls on the telephone. I used various business directories. The reason I believe the telephone is superior is that you are engaging the other party—personally. You can trash a fax or sales letter and delete an unsolicited e-mail. It's a little harder to dismiss a person.

Work on your phone presentation until it's second nature. Practice it. If you're not comfortable on the phone, hire someone who is or hire a telemarketing firm.

<u>Keep good records.</u>

It's important to keep detailed records on your prospects and clients. When I began my career in insurance sales, I was taught a very simple straightforward system of record keeping. It involved using a box of 3x5 lined index cards. The box contained dividers for each month and dividers numbering 1—31 for each day of the month. On the index card I would record information such as:

- ✓ company name
- ✓ company address
- ✓ phone number
- ✓ contact person
- ✓ current insurance plans
- ✓ renewal date

The above entries were pre-printed on my index cards. Each time I made an entry, I would note the date and place it back in the box for an appropriate follow-up.

In recent years I added items like fax number, e-mail and web site addresses.

If a prospect turned into a client, my practice was to create a file on them in addition to the index card.

You can make your system as complex as you like. Years ago, Harvey MacKay created the 66 question Customer Profile. It's mentioned in his classic book *Swim With the Sharks Without Being Eaten Alive.*

With today's technology, desktops, laptops, palm pilots, etc. no doubt there is a more technologically advanced way to store this information. Whatever works for you. If you go the techno route, make sure you save all this important information on a back up system.

A good salesperson is a great interviewer. I remember interviewing America's Sales and Marketing expert, **Tom Hopkins.** I remarked that a good salesperson should ask a lot of questions—just like a good interviewer. Tom totally agreed.

<u>I find that objectionable!</u>

Your prospect is always going to have objections. If you've done your homework or you've simply gone on a lot of sales calls, you know what the objections to your product or service are going to be.

If you're in a sales meeting and your prospect doesn't raise any objections, there are three possible reasons.
1. They're dead.
2. They have absolutely no interest in you or your company. In this case, get out as quickly as you can.
3. They are uncomfortable raising the objection or they haven't thought of it—yet.

Regarding #3, I like to say something like, "You know Mr. Prospect, a lot of companies feel that our price is a bit high, but they come to realize that our service is really a bargain when you consider everything we have to offer." Raise the likely objections if your prospect doesn't—and have a great response at the ready to counter them.

Sales, Marketing and for that matter, Entrepreneurship boil down to one question! What is your Favorite Radio Station? Answer: **WIIFM** (What's **In It For Me?**) Tailor all of your Sales and Marketing efforts to answer that one question. If you answer it well and deliver—you should be successful! Remember, no one likes to be sold—be a consultant.

> *To be a master, you must be a humble student."*
>
> **--Tom Hopkins**

Before I forget, one important aspect of success in business is to always <u>improve</u>. Roy Chitwood, the President of Sales and Marketing International, told me this story. He was once on a plane and he noticed a gentleman who was considered to be a legend in the Life Insurance business—so much so that he was responsible for more production by himself than that of several entire Life Insurance companies combined. Roy went over to the great man and struck up a conversation. Roy noticed that he was reading a book on sales techniques. Imagine, as successful as this man was, he was still interested in improving!

Sales today is more about relationships and consulting. Nobody wants to be sold. You need to establish a rapport with your prospects and a genuine interest in them and their interests and needs.

Anybody that knows me knows that I'm a movie buff. There's a great line from the Tom Cruise vehicle *"Top Gun."* The Top Gun commander (played by Tom Skerritt) is addressing the new class of fighter pilots. **"Gentlemen, you are the Best of the Best—we'll make you better!"** What a great line. Even the best can, and should get better.

One quick tip on marketing materials. Order a small amount of brochures. Why? Because you will want to make a lot of changes. You'll find a better way of saying things. You'll want to add and delete items. Better to pay a little more, than have several hundred brochures that you can't use sitting around.

BARTER YOUR WAY TO SUCCESS

(Save a lot of money and receive thousands of dollars worth of goods and services)

I'm a big believer in bartering. I've bartered a lot of goods and services primarily on my radio show, in lieu of free advertising on my show. I've bartered:

> - Health club memberships
> - Car washes
> - Flowers
> - Ads in magazines
> - Audio Book membership
> - Web design and hosting services

I'm frequently asked my opinions on Entrepreneurship from the Press and Business people. Not so long ago, I introduced the concept of bartering to the young CEO of a local web company. I saw him recently at the gym. He told me that he'd entered into a barter deal with a local 4 star restaurant. He's designing and hosting their web site, and he's receiving thousands of dollars worth of free meals at this fine restaurant. He can bring clients or anyone he wants to impress for an evening of fine dining—for free. Of course, his company has to do the work on the web site—but he has no out-of-pocket costs! Just that one idea on Bartering saved him thousands!

One of the many motivational speakers I've interviewed, **Marcia Wieder**, mentioned on my show that she had always wanted to take a cruise. So she suggested to a cruise line that she would give a lecture on the cruise if they would comp her cruise. They agreed to her proposal. She got a great cruise for free and passengers were treated to a great lecture.

When most entrepreneurs start out, budgets are tight. Obviously, you need cash flow so you can't barter on everything—but it's a great option.

One final tip on bartering. Make sure you hold up your end of the deal. You want the other party to feel like they got a good deal too!

Chapter 8:

HOW DO YOU FINANCE YOUR BUSINESS?

FINANCE OPTIONS

Let's talk a little about Finances. You're going to need money to start your new business. Where do you find it? How about <u>Investors</u>. **Richard Simtob**, President of Talking BookWorld told me a number of his investors were customers who walked into his stores and wanted to know how they could get involved. Of course, most of us don't have stores to show off our wares.

Now <u>Wealthy Investors</u> usually want a piece of the pie—a BIG PIECE. If you put up less than 50% of the money, you may lose control of the business. Wealthy investors are very hard to find. However, lawyers, stockbrokers or bank loan officers may be able to help you. Some may want a fee for that service.

Another source is <u>Friends</u> and <u>Relatives</u>. A word of caution. It can be very dangerous to mix social relationships with business. However, they can be used as endorsers, co-signers or loan guarantors.

You could have a <u>Public Offering of Stock</u>. But the odds are against you. Less than 1% of new businesses can successfully raise capital this way.

<u>Venture Capital</u> is another option. The problem is that they won't talk with you unless you need more than $250,000 and you're in a high growth area like technology. Venture Capitalists want high returns, sometimes as much as 20 times their initial investment within a few years. They reject about 90% of the proposals that are submitted to them because they don't match the technical, geographic or market area of the venture capital group, or because the proposals are poorly prepared. <u>Venture Capitalists usually want significant ownership in your company</u>. According to the National Federation of Independent Business:
- 60% of new businesses are started with personal resources
- 23%-lending institutions
- 9%-friends or relatives
- 3%-investors
- 1%-government
- <1%-venture capitalists

PERSONAL RESOURCES

Let's take a look at Personal Resources. You and your business partners will be the major source of cash in the start up phase. Probably about 50% or more of the total assets will be from personal resources.

Seasoned investors won't invest in a new business unless they know that the owners have made a sizable financial commitment. They know if things get "ugly" you'll be more inclined to "hang tough."

You'll want to put together a <u>Personal Financial Statement</u> that includes: savings, stocks, bonds, loans, credit cards, property, credit, cosigner, life insurance policy, collectibles, etc. You'll probably be surprised at how much you are really worth.

<u>SAVINGS ACCOUNT</u>. A savings account at the bank you're borrowing from is a definite plus. You'll probably have to agree not to withdraw from it during the term of the loan.

<u>CREDIT</u>. Good credit with the bank you are trying to secure a loan from may get you a sizable personal loan.

<u>PROPERTY</u>. Typically, you can borrow up to 75% of the value, less any mortgages.

<u>COSIGNER</u>. An affluent person with an outstanding credit rating can cosign a loan for you. Of course, they become liable should you default on the loan.

<u>LIFE INSURANCE POLICY</u>. If it has cash value it can be offered as collateral for a loan. Generally, you can borrow up to 95% of its value.

<u>COLLECTIBLES</u>. Antiques, art, rare coins can be used to secure a loan.

FINANCIAL INSTITUTIONS

"If you would like to know the value of money, go and try to borrow some."
--Ben Franklin

<u>COMMERCIAL BANKS</u>. To say that Bankers are very conservative is an understatement! It's very hard to find a bank to lend you money to "start a

business." They want to know how and when their money will be repaid, and they want some form of collateral to secure the loan.

CREDIT UNIONS. There are probably several in your area. Originally created to help their members save and make loans to their members at low interest rates, Credit Unions now look for other kinds of investments. If you're having difficulty obtaining funding elsewhere, try a Credit Union.

CREDIT CARDS. Although not the best choice, credit cards can provide you with start-up capital. More than one entrepreneur has started a company by maxing out their credit cards. Credit cards charge a high interest rate but give you 36 months to pay it back.

HOME EQUITY LOANS. Essentially, your home is now a bank thanks to home equity loans. The amount you can borrow depends on your equity in your home. Generally, lending institutions will lend you between 50 and 75 percent of a home's appraised value, minus mortgages. A home loan can be used for any purpose and the interest may be tax deductible. The bank doesn't really care—after all, they have your home as collateral!

There are a couple of basic bank loans to look at. The most common is the Short Term Commercial Loan. This loan is outstanding for 30 to 90 days and is to be repaid once the purpose of the loan has been served: i.e. inventory loan (when the goods are sold.) This type of loan may be unsecured if you have a good credit reputation, or you may be required to provide collateral.

The Long Term Commercial Loan involves the repayment up to 5 years with a monthly schedule. Typical purposes: buying fixed assets, equipment or other items for plant expansion.

Some banks also offer Accounts Receivable Financing. The accounts receivables are put up as collateral. You can borrow 50% to 80% of your customer's debt. In many cases, if your customer doesn't pay you will still have to pay the bank and go after the customer for collection. Many new business start-ups don't qualify for Bank Financing.

As discussed earlier, there are non-bank companies called Factors that extend a line of credit to you based on your Account Receivables. However, the interest rates will be higher. But if you need the money, paying a few additional points to keep your business afloat and help it grow, why not! And as previously mentioned, one of the companies I own—**Premier Funding (248) 258-7760**—can assist you with that type of financing.

<u>What type of bank should you seek?</u> I'd recommend a small, progressive, personal bank. Find one that is hungry for your business. Get to know the bank officers, remember they are human beings too. Personal relationships count! Banks turn down loans for a number of reasons:

- Lack of your ability to repay the loan
- Insufficient equity capital in the firm
- Lack of collateral
- Your character
- Poor business plan

<u>The fact remains that a bank will lend you money if you prove you don't need it!</u> Banks are not in business to lend money—they are in business to make money.

My advice: act as though you want a loan, but do not need a loan. <u>Wanting</u> a loan implies growth and expansion, while <u>needing</u> a loan implies that you are in trouble and may not be able to repay the loan.

Also, call on five or six banks. Ask about current interest rates for commercial loans, general guidelines of acceptance, collateral, repayment methods, etc.

Schedule a meeting with the loan officer. Dress appropriately, make a good impression. Always be truthful on the <u>application</u> and explain any questionable items. On the <u>final interview,</u> bring a business plan and completed application form.

My final point on bank loans is that even if you are turned down, always ask why. What could be done to get a "yes" response? You could resubmit your application or use the information to improve your chances with another lender.

SMALL BUSINESS ADMINISTRATION

The **Small Business Administration** (SBA) offers assistance primarily in the form of guaranteed loans. The loans are made by commercial banks and are guaranteed up to 90% by the SBA. <u>Participation Loans with banks</u>: up to 75% is put up by the SBA and the bank puts up the remaining amount. Other loan programs offered by the SBA include Special Loan Programs, and the little known Lease Guarantee Program (which guarantees the payment of rent to the landlord.)

Other SBA programs:

SCORE (Service Corps of Retired Executives). Relative to finance, SCORE representatives can help you write your business plan at no cost.

SBDC (Small Business Development Centers). SBDC's are affiliated with universities throughout the U.S. They can provide research and assistance for your burgeoning enterprise.

SBIC (Small Business Investment Companies). They provide investment capital, much like a venture capitalist. They are licensed by the SBA PCR (Procurement Center Representatives.) PCR's assist small businesses in getting government supply contracts.

MESBC (Minority Enterprise Small Business Investment Companies). They provide venture capital in minority-owned firms.

SBIR (Small Business Innovation Research). Provides grants as opposed to loans (under SBA supervision.)

Because legislation is constantly changing, programs are added and deleted, my advice is to visit your local Field Office and check out their current programs.

BUSINESS PLANS

"Every well-built house started with a definite plan in the form of blueprints."
--Napoleon Hill

A business plan is simply a roadmap for your business. It will come in handy when you apply for funding from a bank or other lending institution. It need not be long—six to ten pages should suffice, and consists of:

1. Title Page
   States the name of your business, your name, address, phone number and date.
2. Table of Contents
   Lists each topic and corresponding page number
3. Executive Summary
   This section should briefly and clearly state what your business is and how you will run it. You should include business objectives, principal products or services, technology and development program, market and

customers, management team, and financial requirements. Keep it brief (1—3 pages) and interesting.

4. Products or Services
Explain your product or service in detail. Also mention your pricing.

5. Market
Provide a market summary and industry overview. Discuss trends in the market, expected market share, your target customers, and your competition.

6. Marketing
Discuss your marketing campaign: Sales, Advertising, Public Relations, promotions, pricing, and services. Describe your distribution channels. How is your marketing strategy different and superior to your competitors? Set a market share objective, say 20% in the first couple of years.

7. Management Team
Here's your chance to show off. If you or your management team have impressive resumes, list them (especially their successes.) Also list any outside advisors, such as CPA's and lawyers. You might also want to mention incentive plans (stock option and stock purchase plans.)

8. Financial Plan and Forecasts
Your financial plan should explain in detail how much money you will need and how you will pay it back. You should plan for more money than you think you'll need—there's always the unexpected.

Be sure and check out the web sites in the resource section that can assist you with business plans.

Chapter 9:

PICK A CARD, MY CARD!

USE YOUR BUSINESS CARD TO MAKE YOU $$$

With all the latest technology, e-mail, voicemail, faxes, pagers, palm pilots, cell phones, etc., are business cards still effective today? YOU BET!

In this chapter I discuss several strategies and tips that will make you business card savvy! Business cards are great, aren't they? There's a Latin saying, "Cardnito ergo sum." Translation: "I have a card, therefore I am." It's a fantastic feeling to be an entrepreneur and look at your newly printed business cards that say your name and President of the company. They engender a powerful feeling of ownership and independence.

Business cards are great for many reasons:
- They're inexpensive to print.
- You can give them out to everyone.
- You can be as creative as you want to be on your cards.
- You can update them and change them whenever you like.

Of course, business cards will do you no good unless you circulate them. Here are a few business card basics:

Always have business cards on you, wherever you go. You never know where your next opportunity will crop up.
1. You have to get people to read and keep them. Your card should make a great impression. Not only should your card say who you are and what you do, it should leave an indelible impression so they'll think of you in the future.
2. The best time to hand out a card is when someone asks you what you do. If you're talking with someone who you think is interested in your product or service, give him a couple. Hold the card in your hand first and point to what's important on the card. When you do release the card, say something like "this will save you money, hang on to it." Stress how your business will benefit their company.

Business Cards Faux Pas—NEVER:

- Say this is the last card I've got, or worse, hand out someone else's card with your name and number on it.
- Hand out a dirty or bent card.
- Hand out a card from a previous job.
- Say my cell phone number, home phone, web site, e-mail address and fax number are not on the card. Let me write them down for you.

The best way to give and receive business cards—follow the Japanese! They hold their card in front of them with both hands. It's almost a ceremony. They deliver the card with a slight bow. You're expected to do the same. They admire your card and comment on it. You do the same when they hand you their card.

When you receive someone's card, take a moment to look at it. Perhaps write a few brief notes on the back to show your interest in the other person's business. Human nature being what it is they'll probably reciprocate.

If at all possible, offer up a sincere compliment or comment on something on the card. "Oh, I see you're located on 3rd Street. I used to work a few blocks down from you."

Another great time to give out business cards—when you pay bills. Think about it. Most utilities, retail stores, credit card companies provide you with an envelope. Why not include your business card with your payment. Remember, people know people who may have a need for your product or service. Your only cost is a postage stamp!

By the way, should you ever ask for two cards? (You may recall that I suggested giving out two cards if you have a good rapport with the person you're talking with.) It's almost always a good idea to ask for a couple of cards because this may cause the other person to ask for two of yours. If not, it's sure to be taken as a kind and thoughtful gesture.

SORT IT OUT

When you attend a business function where you're going to meet and greet (Chamber of Commerce, trade show, business seminar, etc.) always separate your cards from the cards you collect. It's a good idea to have a suit coat or jacket with several pockets. Keep your prospect's cards in another pocket. Write a brief note on the back of the card as to where you met, their level of interest, etc.

Some great places to display your business cards are bulletin boards at:

- Supermarkets
- Health Clubs
- Restaurants
- Colleges
- Libraries
- Hospitals
- Convenience Stores
- Smaller Shopping Malls
- Social Clubs
- Banks
- Factories
- Bars

BULLETIN BOARDS ARE FREE ADVERTISING

They are especially effective for basic services such as lawn care, tree trimming, professional services and home-based services.

If you use bulletin boards, check back periodically to see if someone has taken your card, or covered it up with one of their own. Obviously, replace your card if it is gone. Give yourself a better position if it's still there. Ancillary benefit: you may must come across someone else's card that you could use.

I use bulletin boards a lot, primarily for my Radio Show. I have an 8½ x 11 flyer for the show which, in addition to listing the times and station, also mentions some of the famous people I've interviewed: **Ed McMahon, Jack LaLanne, Tony Robbins, Jimmy Connors, Mark McCormack, Brian Tracy,** etc.

As a matter of fact, I've put up an autographed publicity photo of myself along with the flyer at a few of the restaurants I frequent. In the autograph I typically say "To my good friends at the ______ restaurant." I usually get some good responses. At one restaurant in particular, **The Star** in Madison Heights, Michigan, the owners frequently say, "People are always commenting on your photo. Many say they went to school with you, or they've heard of you."

Recently I attended a Small Business Seminar in Detroit. Instead of handing out my traditional business card, I brought a folder containing my aforementioned 8½ x 11 radio flyers. While I was talking with someone, I'd ask if I could give them one of my business cards. When they said yes—I'd hand them one of my radio flyers. Their eyes would widen or they'd get a little chuckle. One thing is for sure—I made an impression on them. After discussing the flyer and my show, I'd invariably hand them a regular business card for one of my consulting companies. I picked up a client that day using that technique.

Of course, people probably expect a Radio Talk Show Host to be a little flamboyant. You'll have to judge whether this technique will benefit your product or service.

Here's a little memory trick. When you receive someone's card, comment on their card and say their name. Say their name as many times as you can (without sounding like an idiot.) When I'm sitting across from a new business acquaintance at lunch or dinner, I keep their card on the table in front of me so I can inconspicuously refer to it. If I'm sitting with a few new people, I'll position the cards in the same order as they are seated at the table.

HOW MANY BUSINESS CARDS SHOULD YOU ORDER?

Let's use a simple formula. How many cards do you use in an average week? Let's say your average is 10. Multiply that by 52 (weeks in a year). That's 520. Factor in another 100 for trade shows, conventions you might attend. That's 620.

Why order once a year? Area codes, zip codes change. Maybe you added a fax, e-mail or web site? (You'll need a whole lot more if you follow my business card mini marketing plan that follows.)

NOT YOU AGAIN!

Why not give your business card to the same person, again and again. Let's say you hand out your card to Mr. Jones. Six months later you see him again. Perhaps by now he's lost your card and forgotten all about you. By giving him another card, you have another opportunity to "sell" him on you and your business. Perhaps you moved or added e-mail or a web site. (Let a reasonable amount of time pass before giving your card to the same person.)

I typically put my home phone number on my card as well. I'll tell people that if you can't reach me at the office, try me at home. That tells people that I'm accessible and that I care about their business. Of course, I stress this with my clients.

A variation of the technique is to write your home number on the back of your card in front of your client. That builds a lot off good will.

I've been seen on National Television for about two years in the Carleton Sheets' infomercial. A lot of people will get the number to my radio station or track down my home number. I return a lot of these calls. A lot of people are amazed that someone on National TV would actually take time to call them.

BUSINESS CARD MINI-MARKETING PLAN

You could actually build your business just using your business cards. This is a good strategy, especially if you're on a shoestring budget. Think of it as a mini advertising, marketing plan.

Here's what you do:

- ✓ Send out/hand out a minimum of a dozen cards a day. The first three cards should be sent to people you already do business with. Thank them for their patronage with a brief, hand-written note. Include your business card.
- ✓ Send out three cards to people you'd like to do business with. These are people you've had some previous contact with. Again, send a card and a note mentioning something new that your company is doing that can benefit them.
- ✓ The next three cards should be to names right out of your daily newspaper or subscription magazines. These are people who make news. (I'm frequently written up in the local papers and I receive a lot of calls, many of which become clients.)
- ✓ Give out the remaining three cards to people you have a good rapport with, who might have ideas on how to grow your business.

That's a dozen cards a day. That should take less than an hour a day. Multiply that by 5 workdays a week. That equals 60 cards per week. Now multiply that by 4.3 weeks and you get 300 cards (actually 259) per month. In 6 months you've sent out over 1,500 cards. If just 10% of those cards generate new business—you've added 150 new clients/customers in 6 months!

Chapter 10:

TIME MANAGEMENT—DOES ANYBODY REALLY KNOW WHAT TIME IT IS?

SUCCESSFUL STRATEGIES FOR KEEPING YOU ON TRACK AND ON TIME

Does anybody really know what time it is, does anyone really care? They better, if they want to be successful.

Although I touch on time management elsewhere in the book, I thought it important enough to devote an entire chapter to it. After all, is there a greater resource that we possess than time?

The principles that I will outline in this chapter will benefit the entrepreneur, or anyone who wants to be successful in any walk of life!

Here are a few time-tested strategies for saving you time (and money).

- ✓ <u>Use an appointment calendar, daily planner or electronic organizer</u>.
  I prefer Day-Timers, but you'll need to find a system that works best for you. Find one and stick to it.

- ✓ <u>Handle paper once</u>.
  If it's not important—trash it. If it's something that needs to be acted on at once—act on it, or put it in your "to be done as soon as possible" file. If you use a computer, information can be stored there.

- ✓ <u>Keep your office clean</u>.
  Routinely clean your desk of unnecessary papers. Either file it or get rid of it. If you're not sure about keeping a particular document, store it in a storage area (perhaps a bedroom that's not being used.)

- ✓ <u>Establish your priorities at the beginning of every workday</u>.
  Do your first priority first, and work your way through to the least important.

✓ <u>Establish priorities for the next day</u>.
Each evening as you are winding up the workday, write down on the following day in your business planner what you want to accomplish that day (from most important to least important.)

Rule of thumb for determining a priority: If that particular activity is going to make you money in the near term—that's a priority.

✓ <u>Delegate</u>.
By delegating to others, you multiply your efforts through other people. This is powerful. For example, I respect the power and speed of the Internet. However, I don't have the time nor the desire to spend hours in front of a computer screen. So I engage others to handle it for me.

✓ <u>Multi-task</u>.
My friend, national sales guru **Tom Hopkins** is always doing several things at once. He listens to motivational tapes while he rides his exercise bike in the morning. I find myself multi-tasking quite a bit. As I'm sitting in my den writing this chapter of my book, I'm doing a load of laundry and having someone else tape a TV program for me (on a channel I don't currently have.)

✓ <u>Meetings</u>.
Conduct business meetings over lunch. You gotta eat—make the time effective for you and your guest.

✓ <u>Get a fast computer</u>.
If you're going to get a computer (most of you will or already have one) you may as well get a fast one. Buy the fastest computer you can afford and get plenty of RAM. If DSL or cable modems are available in your area, you should consider signing up. You'll have to balance the increased cost with your increased productivity, effectiveness, and time savings.

✓ <u>Junk Mail</u>.
Speaking of your computer, junk e-mail, sometimes referred to as spam, can be a big time waster. Use your e-mail program to filter out messages from junk senders before you lay your eyes on them. As for old-fashioned, regular junk mail, give it the "deep six."

Make your telephone your friend, not a time waster. We all spend a lot of time on the phone, probably too much time. Here's a few tips to shave minutes, maybe hours, off your phone time and your phone bill.

- If you use a cell phone, don't give out the number. This way you maintain the control.

- Receive and make telephone calls during specific time periods.

- Screen calls or get caller ID. This will save you a lot of time and aggravation.

- Use an Answering Service. That sort of goes back to delegation. They are experts at this. Make sure you get one that sounds professional. Have friends call you there when you first get the service to check on how the secretaries sound.

- If you have a secretary, have that person screen all calls and reroute any that can be handled by someone else.

- Don't play phone tag! Always leave a set time or times that you can be reached.

- If it's an important call, make a list of specific points ahead of time. You may even want to rehearse it a bit beforehand. Tonight Show legend **Ed McMahon** told me that nothing makes a presentation seem as natural as rehearsing it several times. Not only will this technique save you time— it just may make the sale for you. Speaking of Sales, this technique is a must for selling specific products on the phone.

- If you are pressed for time when you receive a call, say something like "You've caught me just as I'm heading out for a meeting. I can give you a minute or two." This will encourage the person at the other end of the line to get to the point.

- Reduce chitchat to a minimum during work hours.

- Meetings—make them count.

TIME SAVING IDEAS ON MEETINGS

- Meetings should only be held if necessary.

- Have a written objective and agenda, and distribute them to all of the participants prior to the meeting.

- Assign a time limit to each person in the meeting. Years ago when I was Director of Marketing for a hospital corporation, my sales meetings were short and sweet. Each sales rep had three minutes to state his or her case.

- Use agenda to keep meeting on track.

- Use food as an incentive to encourage participation in your meetings. Again, people like to eat and hopefully they'll appreciate you for providing them with a meal as well.

- Suggest a beginning and ending time for each meeting—and stick to it.

- Conclude meetings by summarizing key points and standing up at the end.

Whenever you are in your car, turn it into a classroom on wheels. Listen to motivational tapes. If you're low on tapes and would like to hear the success stories of some of America's Best—you can order these tapes at my web site **www.PatrickGilligan.com**. (I know it's a shameful plug—but they really are good tapes!)

21 GREAT WAYS TO WORK LESS—AND MAKE MORE!

1. Always work smart—not hard (unless working hard is working smart).
2. Get a great assistant who will take care of you and help make you look good. Find a loyal assistant and be loyal yourself.
3. Build a financial reserve. Now! Money gives you choices.
4. Become a master at what you do. When you're the best, you decide when you want to work and how much you'll charge. Being the best is about working less and making more.
5. Don't worry about the competition. **Focus instead on being the best you can be.**

6. Limit the number of face-to-face meetings that you attend. Schedule conference calls or video conferences instead. The majority of meetings today would be more productive if you handled them virtually.

7. Stop returning all of your phone calls the same day. Return the important calls the same day and make sure everyone else knows you return most calls within 48 hours. This gives you time to respond rather than react to problems.

8. Stop procrastinating. Rather than putting yet another piece of paper in the piles on your desk, take one of three actions. **Do it. Delegate it. Or dump it.** It's that simple.

9. Delegate.

10. Check your e-mail once a day. But be sure you let people know you check it just once a day. And if you have a bell that rings every time you get an e-mail message, turn it off. I don't want you to act like Pavlov's dogs.

11. Always put yourself first. Everything else is second. If you don't, you'll be too exhausted to add value to anyone's life. Fill yourself up first, and you'll have an abundance to give.

12. Stop hanging out with negative people. They are energy sappers. Align yourself with positive people.

13. Build a support team of experts you can call on for help. If you want to work less and make more, you can't do it all by yourself.

14. Start a habit of calling one person who you respect and admire every week. No, this isn't a call to the same person. It's about cultivating relationships with people that you can connect with once a month. Powerful relationships can bring better opportunities.

15. Pay your bills once a month. And make sure everyone knows you pay once a month. Some people will adjust their billing process to fit yours.

16. Laugh at least 10 times a day. (It's fun and it's a great stress buster.)

17. Stop thinking about all your problems. **Focus on the possibilities instead!**

18. Understand that the real secret to being a Successful Entrepreneur is using your creativity first. Don't worry about what you can't do. Focus instead on what you can do. The answer to your problems is always found in the creative spirit.

19. Exercise. Even if that means going for a brisk walk. Moving your body energizes you. (And you'll look and feel better.)

20. Start to develop multiple sources of income. If you rely on one source, it could dry up. (See Chapter 11.)

21. **Always believe in yourself!**

> *"Money is better than poverty, if only for financial reasons."*
> **--Woody Allen**

Chapter 11:

MULTIPLE INCOME STREAMS

In today's economy, to succeed and thrive we need more than one income stream (source of income). Why you ask? Because when one stream dries up, you'll want to fall back on another.

Let's say you work for ABC Manufacturing. You've worked there for 20 years. One day the plant closes, or is merged with another company and you are "downsized." What then? If you're married, you could live on your spouses income for a while (assuming he/she has a job) and you don't mind seeing your life's savings evaporate.

What can you do to create alternate sources of income? Let's use me as an example. I own an employee benefits consulting company. I help my clients find appropriate Health, Dental, Life insurance plans for their employees. I also work with employee leasing. I receive an ongoing commission from the company whose product I placed as long as the client uses the product. This is the best of all—RESIDUAL INCOME (getting paid over and over again for work you've done once.)

I also derive income from my Radio and Television work. I receive royalties from my Books.

To get back to my previous question, what can you do to create alternative sources of income? The answer—what can **you** do or more to the point, what do **you** want to do?

Many of the same considerations apply to analyzing multiple income streams as you used to determine what business you wanted to start.
- Your own particular talents, skills and abilities
- Your likes and passion

Fortunately, many of these options are discussed in greater detail elsewhere in this book. They include:

- Real Estate

  Buying, fixing up properties and selling them for a profit. Renting out properties. The monthly rent represents residual income.
  - ➢ Part-time Real Estate agent—show homes and make money on the weekends.

- MLM's (Multi-Level Marketing Companies)

  Amway, Mary Kay and NuVision to name just a few. This business can be done on a part-time basis. And again, MLM's offer my favorite component—residual income. I recommend companies that sell a consumable product like vitamins or creams, something that has to be replenished on a regular basis.

- Teach, Instruct

  Perhaps you could give piano lessons, teach computer basics, aerobics? I love tennis. I've been teaching tennis for several local Parks and Rec Departments for over a decade. It's a true win-win for me. I see it as my community service, I get paid for it, and I love it. I take pride in knowing that I've taught hundreds of people, young and old, a great game that they can enjoy the rest of their lives.

  I guess that's the key to teaching: having a passion for it and helping others! That's a great reason for becoming an entrepreneur as well!

- Handyman

  This skill set would lend itself to Real Estate, especially in fixing up properties. But, you could also help people with repairs on the weekends.

- Telemarketing

  Yeah, I hate them too. But if you're good on the phone, you could pick up some dough in the evening and on weekends.

- Books

  If you're an expert on something, write a book. It could be an income source for you. By the way, when you write a book, many will consider you an expert!

- Cross Sell Other Products

  Perhaps companies you work with offer a referral fee or ongoing commission (residual income) on their products or services.

I work with a local PEO (Professional Employer Organization) otherwise known as Employee Leasing. I'll briefly discuss their program with a CEO I'll have on my show or meet at a business function. If they're interested, I'll set up a lunch or meeting with the CEO of the leasing company. If the deal closes, I get a commission for the life of the deal.

I guess I've already said it—but it bears repeating. Find something you love and will genuinely help people. If you can make a residual income, so much the better.

Of course, the bulk of your efforts should be put into your primary business.

Chapter 12:

THE WEB

DO YOU REALLY NEED A WEB SITE?

In a word, YES, if for no other reason than credibility. In the past, when I was talking to a business owner, I'd inevitably ask them if they had a fax number if I didn't see one on their business card. If they said they didn't have one, I'd wonder how serious they were about being in business.

Today, if I'm talking with a business owner and they don't have a web site or e-mail address, I wonder how serious they are about being in business.

Now you'll probably thinking that having a web site for your business sounds great—but isn't it expensive? Yes, however the good news is that starting up and maintaining a web site is easier and less expensive than ever.

Other reasons to have a web presence:
- Nowadays a lot of people turn to the web to find businesses the way they used to turn to the Yellow Pages.
- Some studies suggest that over 50% of homes have Internet access now. More than ever, people are turning to the Internet to check out a business they have heard about.
- One of the biggest reasons to have a web site for your company is what I call "speed marketing." Say you meet or are talking with a prospect on the phone. They say, "Your Company sounds great. Can I get some information on it?" You say sure, check out www.the name of your company. It's almost instantaneous. Heck, I've had people pull up my web site while I was talking to them on the phone!

HOW DO YOU GET A WEB SITE?

If you have the technical expertise and time, you could create one yourself. Most of us don't want to create our own site. Fortunately for us, there are plenty of web site design companies out there. The cost will range somewhere between a couple hundred dollars for a basic site to several thousand dollars for a complex one.

If you want a web site but don't have the expertise, or much money, there is still an option. Find a local high school or college student fluent in HTML (HyperText Markup Language) and pay him (or her) a few bucks to create a site for you.

If you have some expertise and want to try it yourself, there are a number of products out there to choose from. Here are a couple:

- <u>Microsoft FrontPage</u>. This program is very user-friendly and powerful enough to create ambitious sites. It costs about $125.
- <u>WebExpress from Microvision</u>. This is also powerful and user-friendly. It costs about $70.

For those of you contemplating creating your own web site "on the cheap", remember the old adage, *"you get what you pay for."* William Babcock, President and Founder of Advanced Business Technical Solutions, a web design company in Michigan says,

"There is an unfortunate trend resonating among entrepreneurs to generate a company web site at the absolute lowest possible cost. That is, quality and effectiveness become sacrificed with initial fees being paramount. All else is forsaken in deference to price. Far too often we have encountered a client stricken with this widespread parsimonious mindset. When advised that cutting corners in the firm's only worldwide exposure is unsound, it becomes clear that there is a false perception that one web site is the same as another. The reality, however, is in stark contrast to that misguided perception. A firm's web site—whether for a small, medium or large-sized organization—is often the only representation of the business to online visitors. These visitors are not meeting with any staff members, not speaking with anyone via phone, not privy to any other company documentation. Their *only* impression of the business is the company web site. In this case, **the web site IS the business!** When online visitors review the poorly designed web site, proudly developed for the lowest possible amount, the ultimate cost to the business is, in fact, quite high, far from the superb deal they initially sought. Entrepreneurs must realize that producing a cheaply designed web site reflects poorly on any business and its associates.

There are several culprits for the prevalent false assumptions regarding web site design that currently exist. Most prominent is that there are dozens of varieties of web site design software available for a minimal cost. These programs often include template web site designs that the novice can utilize. Of course, web sites designed in this method offer little customization and typically have an amateurish look that is ubiquitous on the web. Another influence on the uninformed regarding web site design is the individual that dabbles in web site design in his or her basement or home office. To contend for a moment that these individuals could produce a shred of the quality that a team of professional designers, artists, writers and programmers could develop is folly. A proper analogy puts the absurdness of a cheaply developed web site in clear focus. If a business was in need of legal counsel to protect them in a criminal or civil matter of even the slightest importance, it is foolish to believe that instead of hiring a licensed attorney, they would opt to purchase off-the-rack legal software and defend themselves. Deeming such a matter far too important to risk a foul-up, the business would clearly forego the inexpensive, do-it-yourself legal software and hire an experienced lawyer for the task at hand. It is difficult to imagine that an organizations only worldwide exposure could be considered any less important."

For further information, you can contact Mr. Babcock at www.abtsonline.com.

HOW GOOD IS YOUR WEB SITE?

Here are a few elements that all effective web sites should contain:

1. Give your visitors a reason to visit and come back, and tell others about your site.

    You've only got a few seconds to hold the attention of a web surfer. If your site is boring—*click* and they're gone. Hold their attention with graphics, photographs, appealing backgrounds. Provide value-added content such as quizzes, news, reports, surveys, etc. How good should it be? An easy way to find out is to check out your competitor's web sites. What do you like about their sites, what don't you like? Ideally, you'll want to create a business site that contains the best and eliminates the worst of your competitor's sites.

2. Dot.com me!

    In addition to registering your web site with the major search engines, Yahoo, Excite, Alta Vista, etc. use a little common sense in picking the name of your site. If you're like me and you own a number of companies and do some other interesting things like host a radio show and appear on national television—use your name. When people ask for information on my show or businesses, I say "Dot.com me. It's all there on my website, www.PatrickGilligan.com." I got this tip from motivational speaker **Denis Waitley** when he was on my show. Make it easy for your clients to find your company on the web. Keep it simple. My funding company is called Premier Funding. If your company is called Jones Plumbing, how about www.JonesPlumbing.com. If they don't know your web site, this will make it easy for clients and prospects to find your site with minimal guessing.

3. Don't let them go, or at least follow them!

   Encourage visitors to your site to give you contact information that you can use in your company's marketing and promotional efforts. Set up a guest book where visitors can leave comments about your site along with their name, title, address, phone number, e-mail address, etc. You could offer to send a complimentary newsletter or e-book to those who provide you with their information. Other ways to get visitor information include contests and special offers.

10 GREAT WAYS TO PROMOTE YOUR WEB SITE

1. Probably the simplest is to include your web address on your business cards, letterhead, faxes, invoices, catalogs, etc.
2. Send announcements on your web site to all of your customers, clients and media. If you really want to make an impression, include a picture of your homepage in the announcement.
3. Mention your web site address on your voice mail system and in your "on hold" message.
4. Whenever you leave a message for someone, especially on a sales call, mention your web site address.
5. If your company has an unusual name or one that is difficult to spell—spell it out on phone messages.
6. Include your web site in all of your advertising.
7. Frequent Internet newsgroups and message boards. Leave messages of your own.
8. Host online chats. Large sites, like America Online, are always looking for knowledgeable hosts who can share their expertise with others.
9. Get registered on the major search engines: Excite, Yahoo, Lycos, HotBot, Alta Vista, etc.
10. Link up with your customers and clients. Also, trade links with companies in your industry that you're not competing with.

OTHER REASONS WHY YOU SHOULD BE ONLINE NOW

1. <u>Your business can be open 24/7/365</u> (24 hours a day, 7 days a week, 365 days a year) because your site is always up.
2. <u>It's cheap</u>. It's one of the least expensive ways to start a business. You could get an inexpensive web site for about $100.
3. <u>Slash your fulfillment costs</u>. Handling orders by phone/mail orders is expensive. Processing your online orders via a web site is cost effective, accurate and fast.
4. <u>Cut staffing costs</u>. A web site can be run by a small number of people.
5. <u>Easy to update</u>. You can update a web site in a few minutes. Think what it would cost to reprint a catalog.
6. <u>Reduce printing and mailing costs</u>. You'll still want to print some materials, but through a web site, your customers can download any information they want.
7. <u>The world is your potential customer</u>. The web is a borderless marketplace.
8. <u>There are no angry customers in your face</u>. Of course, your business success will depend in large measure to effective customer service.
9. <u>There's no city permit requirements</u>. That could all change; however, now there are very few government regulations concerning the web.
10. <u>You control the message</u>. You have control of how and when your message goes out to and is viewed by the world.

ANALYZE THIS!

Do you want to know what the visitors to your site liked/disliked? Check and analyze your web stats. Most web site hosting service providers will provide you with a way to access vital information like: number of visitors each day, where they're from, how long they stayed, pages they viewed, etc

My final advice regarding web sites is to check them often. Regularly visit your site and ask others to view it. You want to make sure it's up and working the way it's suppose to!

Make it easy on yourself. Set your web site as your browser's homepage. This way your web site will come up every time you log on to the Internet.

Chapter 13:

IF YOU'RE YOUNG AT HEART

You're never too young (or too old) to become an Entrepreneur!

I've interviewed a few young Entrepreneurs in my time. I remember interviewing one 16 year old from Boston who owned a Web Design company. He had made about $235,000 and of course he was still in high school!

I've also interviewed Entrepreneurs in their 60's, 70's and 80's. **Paul Harvey** and **Jack LaLanne** were in their mid 80's when I interviewed them. By the way, both of them were sharp as a tack. "Regular" folks, mostly women, in their 60's have appeared on my shows as well.

Let's start with the young. A lot of great entrepreneurs started at a young age. Here are a few:
- Seventeen year old **Fred DeLuca** quit med school to start an obscure submarine shop, currently know as Subway.
- **Michael Dell** sold computer disks out of his dorm room before creating Dell computers.
- **Bill Gates** dropped out of Harvard to create Microsoft.

WHY SHOULD A YOUNG PERSON BECOME AN ENTREPRENEUR?

How about happiness and satisfaction? Many of the young entrepreneurs I've talked to love what they're doing. They find being their own boss to be rewarding and challenging.

As a young entrepreneur, you are not necessarily at a disadvantage. In fact, you probably have an advantage over us old fogies.

- <u>You're Young</u>. Young people are invincible or so they think. They haven't been beaten down by life the way many of us have. When you're young, you have a lot of energy and resiliency, and you can "burn the candle at both ends." It's easier to get advice from established business people. When I was in college, I asked for and got appointments with local business leaders. Most professionals are eager to dispense their sage wisdom to the youthful seekers of wisdom.

I not only use all the brains I have, but all I can borrow.
--Woodrow Wilson

- <u>Mentors</u>. If you're in school, your Alumni Relations office can probably help arrange for you to speak with an alum in the field you are interested in. Who knows, some of these people may become mentors to you.

Disadvantages of Youth:

- <u>Credibility</u>. You're young and you probably look young. Who wants to buy a product or service from a kid who still looks like he's in high school? Answer: a lot of people, if you are passionate and know what you are talking about. Passion sells. So, be passionate and do your homework.

  Another option would be to hook up with an older person (someone older than you). Perhaps make him or her a partner. They could enhance your credibility in meetings and presentations as well as be a sounding board for your ideas.

The Internet has been a boon to the entrepreneur in general and the young entrepreneur in particular. Many of our young people practically grow up on the computer and think nothing of surfing the web.

A lot of the basic advice I give to entrepreneurs is applicable to young entrepreneurs.
- <u>Passion</u>. As I mentioned, passion sells and is infectious.
- <u>Work for someone else</u>. Even if you don't get paid, the experience and knowledge you can acquire are priceless.
- <u>Become an Expert</u>. Read everything you can on your business and field. Take classes and attend seminars. Read major industry journals, newsletters, etc. (Subscribe or go to the library.)
- <u>Get a mentor</u>. Contact Leaders in your chosen field, and make appointments to meet them. Really want to impress them? Offer to take them to lunch.
- <u>Biography</u>. Read up on or watch *A&E's Biography*. (Have someone tape it for you if you don't have cable TV.) Go to school on the most successful people in the world. It will be instructive, educational, and inspirational.

Entrepreneurship is definitely on the rise among younger people. Recent studies indicate that people 25 years and younger are starting a business at a higher rate than any other age group. As a matter of fact, over 35% of companies started between 1995—1999 were started by entrepreneurs under 30.

Some studies suggest that as much as 70% of high school students want to own their own business. If you are among those 70%, and would like to start a business now, or want to learn more about entrepreneurship, there are many schools and universities that offer Entrepreneurship programs throughout the country.

Way back in 1995, *Success Magazine* commissioned a study to determine the best entrepreneur programs. The study determined the top five to be:
1. Babson College
2. Wharton School of Business
3. UCLA
4. Harvard Business School
5. (tie) DePaul University and USC

Another great resource for young entrepreneurs is **SCORE** (Service Core of Retired Executives). These Retired Executives volunteer their time to help entrepreneurs. Make an appointment to see one of them and share your ideas with them. It just takes one great idea!

MOVING ON TO THE MORE MATURE CROWD

Age is really a relative term these days. The population is aging and people are vital at older ages. I previously mentioned **Paul Harvey** and **Jack LaLanne** going strong in their mid 80's. Look at **Regis Philbin**! In his late 60's, he's probably the most popular man on television. The other king of talk, **Larry King**, is as popular as ever at 67!

If you're a mature person, let's say 50 and up, I think you're in a great position to become an Entrepreneur. You have a lifetime of knowledge and wisdom you can only get from life. Perhaps you had tried a business or two in the past and they weren't totally successes. Why not try another one?

Colonel Sanders is a great role model for seniors. We've all heard of him receiving his first social security check at age 65 and setting out to create Kentucky Fried Chicken. What isn't commonly known is that Colonel Sanders had worked in the restaurant business for years, with some successes and some failures. I think that makes him even more of a role model.

He used all of his previous business experiences and lessons learned to form Kentucky Fried Chicken. Why can't you do the same?

Chapter 14:

WRITE IT OFF AND HAVE FUN

You know the old saying "All work and no play...." Being an entrepreneur is serious business; however, there are ways to have fun with your business and have Uncle Sam pick up all or part of the tab!

TAX DEDUCTIONS

Let's take a look at a few legitimate business tax deductions that will allow you to mix business with pleasure.

Need a vacation?

Did you know your company can buy a vacation home that you can personally use a couple weeks out of the year? The catch: you rent out the property to claim all the expenses on the property. Your company can deduct expenses to maintain and repair the property. The opportunity is available under the tax code, so that the depreciation can be taken over a long term (27.5 years).

Typical travel expenses include:
- Transportation costs to and from hotels and airports, car rental, parking costs, and toll fees
- Air, rail and bus fares
- Meals and lodging
- Dry cleaning
- Telephone expenses
- Business entertainment (50% tax deductible)
- Tips

Get away for a day and make it pay! (Or make it a week or two.)

Conventions, Trade Shows, Seminars are deductible IF they are in some way connected with your business. A business day is defined as a day you are required to attend a business-related event. Even Saturdays and Sundays may be considered business days.

We'd all like to get away to Hawaii, San Francisco, New Orleans or Las Vegas for a few days. Plan your next convention, trade show or seminar at one of these great locations and let Uncle Sam pick up part of the tab.

When you plan your next business trip, think about scheduling some vacation time near your destination. The IRS will permit you to deduct the cost of transportation from your home to a destination if the primary purpose for your trip is business. For example, you might spend a couple of days in Orlando at a seminar and a couple of days sight-seeing in Miami. You're entitled to write-off your round trip travel expenses between your home and Orlando as well as hotel bills, meals, etc. during your time in Orlando. However, the expenses you incurred in Miami would be classified as personal and not deductible.

In addition to seminars and conventions, you can generally deduct business trips to visit clients and prospective clients.

Can you deduct your spouse on a business trip?
YES, if your spouse is
- Involved in your business
- Or has business-related tasks at the event

ON A SHOESTRING

If money is tight (it usually is for the first year or two in business), consider staying at a modestly priced hotel around your convention or seminar.

Also, don't forget to take advantage of all the discounts you may have through business associations, credit cards, AAA, etc.

Take a test drive for a week or two! In the market for a new car? Check it out on your next business trip. If you're going to rent a car on your next business trip, and you're considering a new car, why not call ahead and reserve the model you're planning on buying or leasing. If your stay is a week, that's plenty of time to check the car out. And, it's deductible on your business trip!

The key to business travel, or for that matter, any kind of business deduction—*the expenses must be directly related to your business.* If you can document your business-related activities, you should be in good shape with the IRS.

TAKE A CRUISE

Many industries, especially the insurance industry, like to reward their top performers with a cruise to some exotic location. Many companies hold conventions on cruise ships. Are they deductible? Maybe. Look for the words "Tax Deductible" before you sign up, or ask the sponsors if the trip is tax deductible. Generally, you can deduct up to $2,000 provided that these requirements are met:

✓   You have a record of the days and hours of your attendance in business meetings. Get your cruise sponsor to sign your documentation.
✓   The meetings are directly related to the "Active Conduct" of a business.
✓   The ship is registered in the U.S.
✓   The ship travels to ports in the U.S. and it's possessions.

MORE WAYS TO MIX BUSINESS WITH PLEASURE

I love to play tennis. Perhaps you like golf, fine dining, even movies. If your customers like the same things you do—you're in business (*pun intended*). Currently the IRS will let you deduct 50% of entertainment expenses.
Expenses include:

- Country clubs
- Night clubs
- Sporting events
- Meals
- Theaters
- Hunting trips
- Ball games (football, baseball, etc.)

In addition to being tax deductible, there are additional benefits to be derived from attending conferences and seminars.

<u>TRAINS, PLANES AND AUTOMOBILES</u>

As an Entrepreneur, you get a tax break on all the driving you do for business purposes. Your deductions are limited to the actual business use of the car and do not include driving between your home and place of business.

If you own your car, you can either keep track of actual expense or deduct a set amount per mile with the mileage method. If you use the same car for both business and personal use, you must keep mileage records to distinguish between the two.

If you lease a non-luxury car, you can deduct all costs associated with the business use of the auto, including lease payments. The lessee is required to include in gross income an amount based on the fair market value of the car and the percentage of business use.

If you lease a luxury automobile, you can deduct the lease payments. However, you have to add back to your gross income an amount that represents the excess depreciation.

<u>TURN YOUR HOBBY INTO A TAX DEDUCTIBLE BUSINESS</u>

A lot of entrepreneurs start out with a hobby that grows into a business. One of my frequent tips to entrepreneurs is that they love what they're doing and have a passion for it. If you can get paid to do something that you love to do, then you'll never work another day in your life!

If your business activity has generated income, after expenses are deducted, in at least three out of five consecutive tax years, it's generally considered a business by the IRS.

As a practical matter, if you're considering turning a hobby into a business— find out how much you really like it. For example, I love tennis. Over a decade ago, I decided to turn my hobby and one of my great passions into a part-time business. I started teaching tennis for some of the local parks and recreation departments in the summer. I enjoyed teaching tennis and still do. One summer, I decided to run several tennis programs at once. I didn't like it. I guess it was a case of getting too much of a good thing. Another year, I tried my hand at coaching. I was hired to coach the Varsity Tennis team at an elite private school. I hated it! I found out that I wasn't cut out to stand around for hours and watch mediocre tennis. They called me for years to come back and coach. No Thanks. I realized that I'm a hands-on kind of guy. When I teach tennis, I'm constantly giving demonstrations, feeding balls and hitting with my students. Through trial and error, I've determined that running one tennis program in the summer suits me best.

As is practical, experiment with your hobbies. Make sure it's really what you want to do!

KEEPING IT IN THE FAMILY

Nepotism need not be a bad thing—in fact, it can be a profitable practice. Many successful entrepreneurs learned their business, or about business in general, by working in the family business.

Other benefits of nepotism:
- Someday you may want your kids to take over the business.
- Kids can earn money for college or other expenses (as opposed to you just shelling it out).
- You can offer employee benefits (health, dental, life insurance) to family members through your company.
- Hire your parents or even grandparents as subcontractors. Besides providing an income for them, it gives them something to do. Being of value and service is critical to a persons esteem.
- There are limited tax benefits to hiring your kids. One is income splitting. If you own an S corporation, you can reduce your taxes by giving or selling shares to your children. Children under 14 are taxed at their parent's rate on all unearned income over $1,200.
- Give or sell shares to your parents or grandparents who are in a lower tax bracket.

EMPLOYEE BENEFITS (even if they're only for you.)

You have an advantage when you start a business if you are married and receive benefits through your spouse. If you don't have benefits through a spouse, then you'll have to purchase a plan. If you have employees, you are under no legal obligation to offer health or other benefits. However, if your competitors offer fringe benefits and you find yourself in a competitive marketplace, you may have to offer some level of benefits to attract and retain employees.

Self-employed people are entitled to a tax break. They can deduct 40% of health insurance premiums for you and your immediate family. This deduction increases each year to a maximum of 45% in 2002.

As a sole proprietor, you may deduct health insurance premiums for your employees. Incorporated businesses can deduct the full cost of the insurance.

Most business insurance premiums are deductible. Chief among them are:
- Group Health, Dental, Life
- Worker's compensation
- Key pension
- Employers liability
- State unemployment (either as insurance deductions or as a tax, depending on the type of plan your state has.)

Other business tax deductions to consider:
- Phones
- Utilities
- Rent
- Postage
- Internet access
- Retirement plans
- Interest payments on business credit cards
- Education
- Office furniture
- Office supplies
- Business cards

TAX PREPARATION

Let's conclude our discussion of taxes with a few thoughts on tax preparation.

If you plan to do your own taxes, there are some excellent tax software programs like TurboTax for Business, TurboTax Deluxe, Intuit and Kiplinger's TaxCut. TurboTax for Business allows you to choose the correct return for your type of company, and modifies the program accordingly. TurboTax Deluxe is on CD-ROM and has everything you need to file whether you're a business owner or a regular taxpayer. It's EasyStep interview guides you through, questioning and prompting you, filling out the forms, doing all the calculations, and printing the return. These products range from $49.99-$69.99, and are available at most computer software outlets.

On caveat—there are limitations to such programs. If you have a complicated tax situation, the software may not be up to it.

If you decide to pay someone to prepare your business return, you still have to provide the information to your tax specialist. A professionally prepared tax return should be in the $100-$400 price range, although I've heard of some going into the thousands depending on how complicated the return was. Don't forget that having your business tax return done by a tax professional is also deductible.

Chapter 15:

ON THE FRINGE

Let's take a closer look at fringe benefits. As previously mentioned, whether you are a sole proprietor or you employ many, there are a variety of employee benefits to choose from.

HEALTH INSURANCE

Everyone should have some form of health insurance. If you are a one-man band (or one-woman band), it may be a little tougher and more expensive to obtain a quality health insurance plan. There are a number of business associations out there that you can join. The truth is that few of these organizations will actually save you any money on your premiums, although membership in some may entitle you to a richer benefit level than you would obtain on your own. There are also individual health plans that you can purchase whether or not you are in business. Unfortunately, these plans age-rate. So the older you are, the higher the premium. And many of these plans will increase your premium more than once a year, and when you reach a new age group (40, 50, etc.)

One idea is to start your own insurance business or at least obtain an insurance license. Because I am licensed, I sold myself a health insurance plan and I receive a commission on the premium.

There are a few basic types of health insurance. I'll briefly describe each of them.

<u>FEE-FOR-SERVICE</u>

Under this arrangement, a doctor is paid directly for his medical services, either by the patient, or an insurance or government program. Traditional fee-for-service allows people the greatest freedom in choosing doctors and hospitals.

Under a typical indemnity insurance plan, insurance companies agree to idemnify (reimburse) policyholders for a fixed percentage of their medical bills after a payment of pre-established deductible and co-insurance. Typically a deductible will range between $100-$1,000. A typical co-insurance ratio is 80/20, meaning after a patient has met the deductible, then he would be responsible for 20% of the medical bills up to a predetermined amount.

For example, let's say you have the following through your insurance plan:
$250 deductible, 80/20 co-insurance up to $5,000.
You receive medical bills totaling $1,000.

Your deductible	$250
80/20 co-insurance (20% of remaining $750)	$150
You pay a total of	$400

While Fee-for-Service plans do offer the greatest flexibility for patients, they are the most expensive plans because there are few controls placed on them.

<u>MANAGED CARE PLANS</u>
Managed Care is a generic term applied to a system of health care in which medical practitioners are paid a fixed monthly fee to provide a variety of medical services, both preventative and therapeutic. There is a veritable alphabet soup of programs included under the Managed Care banner: HMO, PPO, POS, DMO, etc.

- <u>HMO (Health Maintenance Organization)</u>
  Probably the most well known and often maligned (sometimes rightly so) is the HMO. An HMO is a form of managed care that either operates its own health care facilities (staff model), or contracts with hospitals and doctors to provide health care services (IPA model) at predetermined rates.

  Members receive comprehensive medical coverage plans with an emphasis on prevention. (This component is what drew me to start my first business, a managed care consulting business. I figured, if they keep you healthy, so much the better for everyone!) Usually, patients pay a co-pay for services and prescriptions. Medical providers (doctors, hospitals, nurses, etc.) derive their incomes from the fixed premiums paid by employers and employees.

  Typically, a doctor or medical practice is paid a capitation (fixed amount per HMO patient). They also share in a pool of money set up to cover referrals, diagnostic tests, etc. If at the end of a given period there is any money left over in the kitty, the doctors share in the profit.

  This is where many contend the problem lies with HMOs. Physicians participating in HMO plans have a financial incentive to keep medical procedures to a minimum. If they authorize too many procedures, it could affect their bottom line.

HMOs were and are an answer to the unchecked exploding health care costs of 20 years ago. I believe HMOs have brought quality affordable health care to thousands who otherwise wouldn't of had access to it. Typically HMO plans are less expensive and offer a more comprehensive range of benefits.

The biggest drawback to HMOs is: you must use a doctor or provider who participates in your HMO. That's an insurmountable obstacle for some people.

- PPO (Preferred Provider Organizations)
     If Fee-for-Service plans lack control and HMO's offer too little choice in picking a physician or hospital—PPOs are viewed as a compromise.

     A PPO is a hybrid of a Fee-for Service plan and an HMO. If you stay within the PPO's Network of doctors and hospitals, you receive a rich benefit (like an HMO). If you stray outside the Network, you receive a lesser benefit (like a Fee-for-Service plan).

     Typically, HMO plans are the least expensive of the three, followed by PPO and Fee-for-Service.

- POS (Point of Service)
     A POS is like a PPO or an HMO? (Frankly, I get confused and I've owned a managed care consulting business for years.) Actually, a POS allows you to bypass your Primary Care physician (under a strict HMO arrangement, you must pick a physician known as your Primary Care physician or gatekeeper for your primary medical services) and go directly to a specialist.

- DMO (Dental Maintenance Organization)
     A DMO is also referred to as DHMO (Dental Health Maintenance Organization). Essentially, dental plans are set up like health plans these days (Fee-for-Service, Managed Care, etc.)

A few considerations when picking a health care plan:
1. HMO's are usually best for people with young families because exams, checkups, doctor visits, and immunizations are typically covered with a nominal co-pay.
2. If you have some medical concerns and you want to use a particular doctor or hospital, a Fee-for-Service or PPO plan may be better for you.

These days most physicians and hospitals belong to one or more of these plans, so check out the plans in your area.

3. Costs. The premiums you pay for coverage are only the tip of the iceberg. Take a closer look at your other costs—co-pays, deductibles, co-insurance, prescriptions, etc.

Related health care coverages included:

<u>DENTAL</u>. As previously mentioned, dental plans come in all shapes and sizes just like health plans. Compare costs vs. benefits, providers, etc.

<u>VISION CARE</u>. Vision care plans typically pay for eye exams, glasses or contacts (to some degree). There are also Fee-for-Service and Managed Care variations of these plans as well.

NOTE: Both Dental and Vision as well as other products can be offered on voluntary basis whereby the employees pick up all or part of the cost.

SLASH YOUR HEALTH CARE COSTS
(or at least cut them down to size.)

In addition to joining business associations, local Chambers of Commerce or professional groups may also offer some type of discount.

Increase your deductible or co-pays. This is probably the easiest and most direct way to decrease your insurance premiums. By increasing your deductibles and co-pays, you could possibly save up to 50% on your premiums.

Many larger companies "self insure" their medical coverage. They hire a TPA (Third Party Administrator) to administer their plan. The company and TPA agree on a stop loss amount (a dollar amount at which point an insurance company steps in and starts paying claims.)

If you are a single sole proprietor in reasonably good health—you could in essence, self insure yourself. That is, you could select a very high deductible and a less moderate co-insurance (say 50/50 as opposed to the standard 80/20). This would significantly lower your premiums and, of course, your medical coverage. You'd essentially be using your insurance policy as a "Stop Loss" or a "Catastrophic" plan. You could conceivably save thousands over the course of a few years. If one year you incurred a lot of medical bills—it could cost you thousands. It's a roll of the dice!

TO LEASE OR NOT TO LEASE?
(actually that's the wrong question.)

There is a surprising amount of misinformation out there about Employee Leasing. A lot of sources, including supposed experts on business, confuse Employee Leasing with Temporary Employment Agencies.

In part to lessen the confusion, Employee Leasing Companies are now called Professional Employer Organizations (PEO). PEO's carry out the administration of having employees. As the employer, you still hire and fire personnel, and direct your work staff just as you would if a PEO wasn't involved.

PEO's can be a valuable tool for entrepreneurs. You're not in business to deal with personnel related issues, such as payroll and employee benefits. PEO's handle these burdens for you and in many cases, can actually save you money on employee benefits, MESC, SBT, etc. And through a PEO, you can obtain access to benefits, such as cafeteria plans and retirement plans that you wouldn't normally have access to.

OTHER FRINGE BENEFITS TO CONSIDER

When you start a business and for some time after, you may not have a steady income. The basic forms of **income protection** are:

DISABILITY INSURANCE. This insurance pays a percentage of your income to you in the event you become sidelined due to illness or injury. This form of insurance is available in either short or long-term policies. It is expensive for individuals.

WORKERS COMPENSATION. Required by law if your company has three or more employees. It provides a fixed amount of income to workers injured on the job. Many health insurers will not provide health insurance to your company without proof of workers compensation.

UNEMPLOYMENT INSURANCE. Required by Federal and State law of employers with one or more employees for at least 20 weeks in a calendar year. This insurance provides a fixed amount of income for employees who lose their job through no fault of their own.

Workers Compensation and Unemployment Insurance should only be considered if you hire employees. Disability Insurance should be considered along with health insurance.

<u>LIFE INSURANCE</u>.
There are hundreds of life insurance companies that want to sell you some type of life insurance. Basically, a life insurance policy pays whomever you designate as your beneficiary a lump sum of money when you die. There are a variety of life insurance products to choose from including term, universal, and whole life.

If you are an individual with no dependents or partners, I'd recommend getting a TERM LIFE policy. It's the cheapest form of life insurance and I'd suggest getting just enough to cover your final expenses. Many health insurers include inexpensive term insurance in their health policies. If you have a spouse, you may want to consider Dependent Life Insurance. For a nominal amount it provides coverage for your spouse.

If you have employees, you'll want to consider offering GROUP TERM Life Insurance to them. The first $50,000 of coverage is a tax deductible expense to your business if the premiums are 100% company paid. You could also make life insurance coverage available to your employees at their expense.

If you have a partner or partners, you should consider a Key Man policy to insure the lives of Key executives or a buy-sell agreement.

<u>CAFETERIA PLANS</u>
As your business grows and you add employees, the cost and variety of benefits you may provide them grows as well. Instead of providing everything for everybody, you can let them pick and choose among a variety of benefits. With a Cafeteria Plan, the employee is offered a menu of various fringe benefits the company is providing—typically health insurance, dental insurance, disability insurance, group term life insurance, disability insurance, vacation days, day care and group legal services. This way, you're only paying for the benefits they pick and you're paying for part of the cost in pre-tax dollars.

BE FLEXIBLE. A flexible spending account provides non-taxable benefits. With this plan, an employee can receive reimbursements for certain expenses, usually medical expenses, dependent care or legal services.

<u>RETIREMENT AND SAVINGS PLANS</u>
Some Financial Planners suggest that Social Security benefits will account for about 1/3 of the income one would need in retirement. Some think a third is optimistic. In any case, as an Entrepreneur, you will have to provide for your own retirement. Here are a few options to consider:

<u>Simplified Employee Pension (SEP-IRA)</u>

This plan is ideal for a home-based entrepreneur and may be adopted by a sole proprietor, partnership or corporation. SEPs are easy to set up and can be maintained with little paperwork. The most attractive aspect of a SEP is that you are allowed to contribute up to $30,000 or 15% of your business's net income per year—whichever is less.

<u>KEOGH</u>

Keogh's or HR-10 plans offer the highest limits for tax deferred contributions; however, they are complicated to set up and maintain. There are two types:

- <u>Defined Contribution Plan</u> may be a profit sharing plan which lets you put away 15% or $30,000, whichever is less.
- <u>Defined Benefit Plan</u> attempts to pay out a particular sum of money each month in retirement. Contributions are limited to the amount needed to eventually produce an annual pension payment of the lesser of $130,000 or 100% of your average compensation for your three highest years.

<u>401K</u>

The 401K Retirement Plan may be offered in a cafeteria plan. You and your employees decide whether to receive cash or have a set amount contributed to a qualified profit sharing or stock bonus plan. Company contributions are deductible and not taxed until withdrawn from the plan. Tough discrimination rules apply.

There are a variety of other Fringe Benefits that you can offer your employees:

- Employee Stock Option Plan (ESOP)
- Thrift Plans
- Profit Sharing
- Savings Incentive Match Plan (Simple)

Chapter 16:

WHAT KIND OF BUSINESS ENTITY SHOULD YOU OPERATE UNDER?

Now that you've done your market research, you have an available product or service to take to market. What kind of Business Entity should you operate under? Should you be sole proprietor or form a corporation?

Before we go any further, let me state that I am not an attorney or a CPA. However, I believe I can give you a practical overview of each entity. Consult a CPA or attorney for specific questions.

SOLE PROPRIETORSHIP

The simplest form of business ownership is the Sole Proprietorship. Some jurisdictions require that you fill out a DBA (Doing Business As) paper. That's it! When I created my health care consulting business, I had some business cards, envelopes and letterhead stationary printed up and I hired an inexpensive answering service. Voila, I was in business! The main disadvantages are that you are personally liable for your company and you must pay the full self employment tax. Other advantages are that you are in total control, and you don't have to share your profits with anyone. Pursuant to legislation enacted in 1995, sole proprietors may deduct up to 45% of their health insurance premiums through 2002 in calculating their adjusted gross income. And that percentage is going up every year.

PARTNERSHIP

One step up in complexity is the Partnership in which two or more people act as joint proprietors. They provide joint funding, joint management and joint financial responsibility. Like a sole proprietorship, the partners are personally liable to an unlimited degree for all the other partners errors.

CORPORATION

A Corporation is the most sophisticated and protective form of business ownership. It is essentially a "legal person" completely separate from the individuals who own and control it. A corporation has the power to do just about anything a person can: own property; lend and borrow money; sue; and be sued, etc. Most importantly, it offers its shareholders limited liability. Its stockholders can lose no more than their original investment. They are not liable for the debts of the corporation.

Other benefits of incorporating include purchasing employee benefits out of pre-tax dollars. These include medical, life, and disability insurance. And you have greater pension benefits—Keogh, 401K, etc.

Probably the biggest disadvantage to incorporating is double taxation. You will have to pay two taxes—corporate and personal. Your corporate profits are first taxed at the corporate level and then your own personal level when your corporation pays you a dividend.

When does it pay to incorporate? The real benefits start when you're earning around $30,000 a year. At $30,000 net taxable income, single entrepreneurs are in the 28% bracket. However, if they draw a salary of $20,000 instead and retain $10,000 in the corporation, they are taxed at approximately 15% on the $20,000 and the corporation is taxed at 15% on the $10,000. For married people, real tax advantages start around $40,000 net taxable income. There is a lot more paperwork and planning involved when you incorporate. Regular business corporations are referred to as C Corporations.

S CORPORATION

S Corporations are a popular form of business entity. In an S Corp, profits and losses flow through to the individual shareholders and profits are taxed as personal income. In a C Corp, you choose whether corporate profits remain in your corporation or are paid to you. Who benefits most from S Corps? Generally, professional corporations and corporations whose chief source of income is consulting or the performing arts. The ideal S Corp candidate is: single; with few medical expenses that total less than $1,000 a year; a member of a perilous profession (which the IRS defines as corporations whose principal function is "services in the field of law, health, engineering, architecture, accounting, actuarial science, performing arts, or "consulting"); faces flat tax rate of 35% if doesn't elect S Corporation status; who needs most of corporate income to live on; doesn't care about income splitting; and is indifferent to borrowing from a pension fund, which is prohibited in S Corporations. Contrast that with the ideal C Corp candidate who is: married; with heavy medical expenses over $10,000 a year; not a member of a perilous profession; entitled to corporate tax rate of 15% on income under $50,000; does not need most of corporate income to live on; plans to take advantage of income splitting; and who plans to borrow from the pension fund in several years to buy a new house.

LIMITED LIABILITY COMPANY

Another very popular business entity is the Limited Liability Company (LLC). An LLC is a non-corporate form that combines the limited liability of a corporation with the flow-through tax treatment of the partnership. Generally LLC's require two or more owners, although some states require only one.

Folks, I hope I've given you a general overview of the various forms of business ownership. For more detailed information, included at the end of this chapter are a couple of charts for you to review. Please consult an attorney or CPA for specific information.

TYPES OF BUSINESS ENTITIES

	CONTROL	LIABILITY	TAX	CONTINUITY
SOLE PROPRIETORSHIP	Owner maintains complete control over the business.	Owner is solely liable. His/her personal assets are open to attack in any legal case.	Owner reports all income and expenses on personal tax return.	Business terminates on owner's death. Owner can sell the business, but will no longer remain the proprietor.
GENERAL PARTNERSHIP	Each partner has the authority to enter contracts and make business decisions, unless the partnership agreement stipulates otherwise.	Each partner is liable for all business debts.	Each partner reports partnership income on individual tax return. The business does not pay any taxes as its own entity.	Unless the partnership agreement makes other provisions, a partnership dissolves on death or withdrawal of a partner.
Limited Partnership	General partners control the business.	General partners are personally responsible for partnership liabilities. Limited partners are liable for the amount of their investment.	Partnership files annual taxes. Limited and general partners report their share of partnership income or loss on their individual returns.	Death of a limited partner does not dissolve business, but death of general partner might unless the partnership agreement makes other provisions.
LIMITED LIABILITY COMPANY	Owner or partners have authority.	Partners are not liable for business debts.	Partners report income and income tax on their individual tax returns.	Different states have different laws regarding the continuity of LLCs. In some states, LLCs dissolve on death or withdrawal of an owner.
C-Corporation	Shareholders appoint board of directors, which appoints officers, who have the highest authority.	Shareholders generally are responsible for the amount of their investment in corporate stock.	Corporation pays its own taxes. Shareholders pay tax on their dividends.	The corporation is its own legal entity and can survive the death of owners, partners and shareholders.
S-Corporation	Shareholders appoint board of directors, which appoints officers, who hold the highest authority.	Shareholders generally are responsible for the amount of their investment in corporate stock.	Shareholders report their shares of corporate profit or loss in their individual tax returns.	The corporation is its own legal entity and can survive the death of owners, partners and shareholders.

COMPARISON OF BUSINESS ENTITIES

	Sole Proprietorship	Limited Liability Partnership	Limited Liability Co.	C Corporation	S Corporation
LEGAL LIABILITY	Unlimited	Limited	Limited	Limited	Limited
Tax Filing	On form 1040: Schedule C Schedule SE	Form 1065 Distributes K-1s to Shareholders	If one member: taxed as sole proprietor If Corp status: Form 1120	Form 1120	Form 1120S Distributes K-1s to Shareholder
TAXABLE YEAR	Calendar Year	Calendar Year	Usually Calendar Year	Fiscal or Calendar Year	Calendar Year (with rare exceptions)
Taxation of Income	Directly to owner on Form 1040 Proprietor also pays 15.3% self employment tax.	Taxed directly to Shareholders on Form 1040. All income is self employment taxable at 15.3%.	Like Sole Proprietor or C Corporation	Taxed first at corporate level and again at shareholder level if distributions (dividends) are distributed.	Taxed directly to Shareholder on Form 1040. No double taxation.
Employment Taxes	Proprietor pays 15.3% self employment tax.	Wages are subject to employment taxes.	Like Sole Proprietor or C Corporation	Wages are subject to employment taxes.	Wages are subject to employment taxes. May use distributions to avoid some employment taxes.
TAX PAYMENTS	Proprietor makes estimated quarterly tax payments.	Shareholder makes estimated quarterly tax payments.	Like Sole Proprietor or C Corporation	Wages are subject to withholding.	Wages are subject to withholding. Shareholders may need estimated quarterly tax payments to cover distributions.
RETIREMENT PLANS	IRA, KEOGH, SEP	IRA, KEOGH, SEP, SIMPLEs	IRA, KEOGH, SEP, SIMPLEs	Profit Sharing, ESOP, SEP, SIMPLEs	Profit Sharing, ESOP, IRA, SIMPLEs

Chapter 17:

VISUALIZATION

Is it necessary to be a great visionary to be a successful Entrepreneur?
I would say YES!

Henry Ford envisioned a car in every driveway. (They probably didn't
have driveways back then, but you get the idea.)

Bill Gates envisioned a computer in every home.

Even a little entrepreneur like me believed that the future of health care
in the 80's was HMO's.

When I first began my radio show in Michigan, some four years ago, I used a
form of visualization. I set three seeming impossible goals for myself:

1. To be seen on National Television everyday
2. To Host a National Television program
3. To Host my own National Television program

Well, I've been on National TV everyday for over two years and I've Hosted
a National Television program as well! Two out of Three Ain't Bad! Maybe
not—but I still want to Host my own National TV Talk Show. And I will
someday!

By the way, I announced these goals to the local media and it has appeared in
the local press many times. I think that 's a great motivator right there—when
you tell someone about your goals, you're obligated to achieve them!

All great athletes use visualization. They see themselves making the perfect
putt, throwing the perfect pass or hitting the perfect serve. Olympian **Bruce
Jenner** visualized every movement of every event to win his events.

CAN YOU BE A VISIONARY?

Sure. Why not!
Here are a few practical tips you can use to become a visionary.
Keep a pad and pen on your nightstand by your bed. Sometimes I'll go to
bed and my mind will unconsciously be working on a problem from earlier that

day. When you wake up in that situation—get up and write down your ideas. They'll be some of your most imaginative! Sure beats counting sheep.

If you want to actively try to visualize, try this.
1. Go to a room where you will not be disturbed.
2. Find a cozy, comfortable chair where you can relax—away from the phone and other distractions.
3. Put on some classical music. Studies suggest that classical music can put your mind in a creative state.

    (I often put on classical music when I'm working on a creative endeavor, or when I just want to think.)
4. Turn down the lights, close your eyes, and let your mind wander.
5. Breathe in and out slowly a few times to attain maximum relaxation. When you are deeply relaxed, you are at the Alpha Level—you're now connected to your subconscious mind.
6. Start to see with your mind's eye. Picture what you want—an upcoming meeting going smoothly, the kind of car you want, the house you want, phone conversations going smoothly. In short, picture yourself as successful!
7. Make an affirmation mentally and verbally. **"I will succeed, I will meet my goals."**
8. See Long Term Goals as well. See yourself driving that luxury automobile you always dreamed about or being on the cover of *Success Magazine*. Whatever your goals are—see them happening!
9. Get the feeling that you are already achieving right now what you want. Legendary motivational speaker, **Brian Tracy** recently told me of a simple technique he's been teaching for years. Take out a sheet of paper and make a list of ten things that you want to accomplish in the next year. Write them down as though you've already achieved them. Example—"I made $100,000" or "I appeared on the Tonight Show." Brian swears by this technique.

Visualization is **POWERFUL**. It's really the start of all great ideas! Just five minutes a day, early in the morning when you first get up or whenever you think best, can transform your life!

Chapter 18:

CONCLUSION

Ladies and Gentlemen, I believe I've covered the key aspects to becoming a Successful Entrepreneur. I defined entrepreneurship; provided a test to determine if you have the traits necessary for success; touched on Hot Businesses; discussed the pro's and con's of buying an existing business, real estate, franchise, mail order, multi-level marketing companies; marketing; advertising; finance; market analysis; types of business ownership; and when to start a business. I hope my advice has been practical and helpful.

I'd like to conclude this book with a few more pragmatic thoughts and to reiterate something I said earlier. <u>There is NO magic, get rich business</u>. They all have their pro's and con's. It all comes down to your unique skills, talents and likes. Once you determine what business to start, make sure your product or service is something people want and are willing to pay for. Then look long term. Is your product something that people will need 5, 10, 15 years from now? Example: Real Estate. Do people need a place to live? Yes. Will they need a place to stay 10, 15, 20 years from now? Probably.

Don't take crazy risks. Successful entrepreneurs take calculated risks. **Mark McCormack**, President of International Management Group (IMG) who created the whole sports marketing industry some 30 years ago on a handshake with Arnold Palmer, told me that had that not worked out with Arnold, he still had his law practice to fall back on. By the way, Mark's advice on my show was in part *"to be honest, dependable, and punctual."* That's pretty good advice.

Enlist the support of your spouse, friends, and family. It's crucial to your success. If through an unfortunate event, such as being fired from a job, you are more or less forced into becoming an entrepreneur, don't despair. Embrace the opportunity. **Carleton Sheets**, probably this country's preeminent expert on Real Estate, got involved in real estate investing because he lost his job. And I think he's done pretty well!

I also think it's important to have a positive frame of mind. How do you do that? Listen to motivational tapes, read motivational books, etc. It's also good to have one or two of what I call "Cheerleaders" in your life. These are people who totally believe in you and your cause. These are folks that on your worst days, when the world has just hammered you, you can call and they'll make you feel like a million bucks! Recently I heard from a dear friend who I hadn't talked with in a while. I had just walked in and was checking my messages on the answering machine. So I hit the button and heard "Pat, this is Bill. I just saw this clean cut, honest looking guy on television. Pat, if you don't make it to the Big Time, there is no God in heaven!" I can't tell you what that meant to me.

I can't stress this enough. Find something that you love to do. Life is too short to do something that you hate!

During an interview with one of the great motivators of our time, **Anthony Robbins**, I briefly discussed with him my success in broadcasting and asked him to comment on it. He said, "You've done the most fundamental thing for success, which is:

- Find your passion
- Focus on it daily
- Move ahead with some form of action
- Adapt to whatever occurs

And you tend to achieve what you want." I think that's great advice for success as an Entrepreneur—or any worthwhile endeavor!

Make sure you have a regular exercise program in place. You'll need to be fit to meet the rigors of entrepreneurship and enjoy its benefits.

My final thought is always believe in yourself. Remember how many times Mark Victor Hansen and Jack Canfield, the authors of the now famous "Chicken Soup for the Soul" book series were rejected before they found a publisher that would publish their books. Think of how many people rejected Colonel Sanders and Henry Ford. Ford's path to building his car had many detours and dead ends. "No man of money even thought of it as a commercial possibility," Henry Ford once wrote. His business manager, James Couzens, once said Ford was thrown out of so many offices in Detroit, that one time he just sat on a curb and openly wept! I believe Mr. Ford eventually found some success in the Automobile Business.

My final, final thought is always keep your word. If you say you're going to do something, do it! People respect integrity. I recently heard a speaker say that people stop dreaming by age 25. Never stop dreaming. I believe **Winston Churchill** said, "Never, Never, Never, Never give up." That's good advice.

Remember folks, **"If you can imagine it, you can achieve it. If you can dream it, you can become it."** **I'm Patrick Gilligan. I'll see you next time!**

WINNERS

W Work. Winners *work* smart, not hard (unless the situation calls for working hard).

I Intuition. Winners rely on their *intuition* to guide them.

N Now. Like Nike says, *"Just Do It!"*

N Natural Talent. Winners rely on their *natural talent* and delegate the rest.

E Energy. Winners have abundant *energy* to accomplish their goals.

R Repeat. Winners *repeat* what works and discard the rest.

S Sell. Winners always *sell* themselves first, their products and services after.

RESOURCES

BUSINESS ASSOCIATIONS

American Home Business Association
http://www.homebusinessworks.com/

American Marketing Association
www.ama.org
250 South Wacker Drive, Suite 200, Chicago, IL 60606
312-648-0536

Association of Small Business Development Centers
www.asbc-us.org

American Small Business Association (ASBA)
www.asbaonline.org

American Society of Inventors
P.O. Box 58426, Philadelphia, PA 19102
215-546-6601

Chambers of Commerce
http://chamber-of-commerce.com

Direct Marketing Association
www.the-dma.org.

Disabled Businesspersons Association
Helps disabled entrepreneurs and professionals maximize their potential in the business world and encourages workforce participation by the disabled
www.web-link.com/dba/dba.htm

Independent Business Alliance
Organization established to give small business owners and home-based entrepreneurs the same purchasing power as large companies
www.ibaonline.com

International Small Business Consortium
Extensive database of small businesses from around the world-with numerous web links
www.isbc.com

Links to many other Business and Trade Associations
www.investoralert.com/link6.html

National Association for the Self-Employed (NASE)
   Group purchasing, legislative monitoring, and advice.
www.nase.org

National Association of Women Business Owners (NAWBO)
Nawbostl@ibm.net
888-569-9813, 314-436-2223
Fax 314-436-1176

National Business Incubation Association (NBIA)
www.nbia.org
1 President Street, Athens, OH 45701
740-593-4331

National Foundation of Independent Business (NFIB)
www.nfidonline.com
600 Maryland Ave. SW, Suite 700, Washington DC 20024
202-554-9000

National Venture Capital Association (NVCA)
www.nvca.org

Sales and Marketing Executives International
www.smei.org

SCORE (Service Corps of Retired Executives)
www.score.org

Small Business Administration Office of Womens Business Ownership
409 3rd Street SW, 6th Floor, Washington DC, 20062
202-205-6675

Small Business Center of the Chamber of Commerce
1615 H. Street NW, Washington D.C., 20062
202-659-6000

Trade Show Central
   Free info on over 10,000 tradeshows worldwide.
www.tscentral.com

Working Today
National nonprofit membership organization that promotes the interests of freelancers, including people working from their homes.
www.workingtoday.org

<u>FOR THE YOUNG ENTREPRENEUR</u>
An Income of Her Own (AIOHO)
PO Box 987, Santa Barbara, CA 93102
805-687-0983

Junior Achievement (JA)
www.ja.org
719-540-8000

National Association for Teaching Entrepreneurship (NFTE)
508-758-6411

Young Entrepreneurs Organization (YEO)
www.yeo.org
703-527-4500

BUSINESS PLANS

<u>Business Plans</u>
www.businessplans.org
www.bizplanit.com/free.htm
www.bplans.com/start.cfm
www.brs-inc.com
www.jian.com
www.morebusiness.com/templates_worksheets/bplans/
www.palo-alto.com/demos/demos.cfm
www.sb.gov.bc.ca/smallbus/workshop/busplan.html
www.sba.gov/starting/indexbusplans.html

Small Business Advancement Center
List of colleges that offer free or low cost assistance with business plans.
www.sbaer.edu
501-450-5300

Small Business Success
> *Published by the SBA and Pacific Bell, this booklet discusses business planning and marketing*
> 800-848-8000

CHECK ON THE COMPETITION

Better Business Bureau
> *Find information from the Better Business Bureau*
> www.bbbonline.com

Direct Selling Association
> *If you're unsure about a direct selling opportunity*
> www.dsa.org

Marketers
> *Check out your competitor's web sites here.*
> www.advert.com

<u>Research you competition</u>
> www.yahoo.com
> www.excite.com
> www.hoovers.com
> www.bigbook.com
> www.companiesonline.com
> www.prars.com
> www.businesswire.com
> www.sjmercury.com   *(computer industry)*
> www.washingtonpost.com   *(government)*
> www.latimes.com   *(entertainment industry)*
> www.companysleuth.com
> www.creditifyi.com
> www.knowx.com
> www.thomasregister.com

> to track specific trends in targeted industries
> www.voxcap.com
> www.pointcast.com

E-BUSINESS

Biz Rate
Evalulates e-tailers.
www.bizrating.com

Commercenet
www.commercenet.com

E-Commerce Research Room
Over 1,500 reports and resources focused on e-commerce
www.webcommercetoday.com/research/

E-Commerce Times
www.e-commercetimes.com

Electronic Commerce Guide
E-commerce information for both beginners and experts
http://ecommerce.internet.com/

E-marketer
Stats, facts and tips about selling online
www.emarketer.com/

Profit Tips
If you are into marketing your own products or services, visit Profit Tips-your best source for e-business knowledge
www.profittips.net

Yahoo E-Commerce
http://smallbusiness.yahoo.com/smallbusiness/ecommerce

Yahoo! Store
Build an online store
http://store.yahoo.com

FINANCING

America's Home Business Funding Directory
www.businessfinance.com/

Finding money on the Web
www.quicken.com/banking_and_credit
www.ventura.com
www.garage.com *(matches up investors with home-based businesses)*

National Credit Systems
An accounts receivable management firm, with a collection system that increases recovery rate, lowers collections costs & improves cash flow.
http://nationalcredit.com

National Venture Capital Association
www.nvca.org/

Private Investor Network
www.investoralert.com/link6.html

SBA—Financing Your Business
www.sba.gov/financing/

Small Business Finance
Find the best bank rates for loans, credit cards and savings
www.bankrate.com/brm/biz_home.asp

Small Business Service, Expanding Internationally
Resource for importers and exporters
http://home3.americanexpress.com/smallbusiness//segments/expand_intl.asp

Stock Quotes
Track stock movements.
www.quote.com

Venture Capital Firms
Benchmark
www.benchmark.com
Business Angels
www.business-angels.com/us/index.html
Kleiner, Perkins, Caufield & Byers
www.kpch.com
Venture Capital Resource Library
www.vfinance.com

FORMING/RUNNING A BUSINESS

American Incorporators
Provides a comprehensive range of services to businesses wishing to incorporate in the United States.
www.ailcorp.com

Business Filings Inc.
Company that will incorporate small businesses in the U.S. and offshore for a fraction of the cost of using an attorney.
www.bizfilings.com

Company Corporation
www.corporate.com

Corporate Creations
www.corpcreations.com

IncorporateTime
www.incorporatetime.com

Parcorp Services
Online incorporation, LLC formation, and registered agent services.
www.parcorpsvcs.com

Schedule C.com
An online resource for sole proprietors and anyone running a small business. Extensive list of resources and links.
www.schedulec.com

FREEBIES

Catalog Savings
Catalog Savings.com lets you order unique catalogs for free! Save money with exclusive online savings certificates
www.catalogsavings.com

Downloads
Click on the business link for all sorts of business related programs, professional contracts, etc.
http://download.cnet.com

E-mail
For busy executives. Available every day, 7 days a week, world wide.
www.ethailand.com

E-organizer
Keep online to-do lists, appointment schedules, birthday lists, etc.-and get email reminders when the dates near.
www.eorganizer.com/

Free stuff
Some of the free stuff includes electronics, jewelry, toys and much more up to 100 percent off. Free after rebate!
www.broketoo.com
The most comprehensive directory of free stuff, sweepstakes and trial offers on the Internet. Don't pay for it when you can get it for free.
www.freebiefarm.com
The Web's premier free stuff! CD-roms, downloads, software, catalogs, magazines and more!
www.freetown.net

Pre-Retirement
Prepare for the golden years! Send for your free retirement booklet
www.the-golden-years.net

Print
Get printing jobs, announcements, labels, notepads, business stationery and more.
www.iprint-1.com

Software
Clip Art
www.free-clip-art.com
Shareware.com
The place to find "try before you buy" software
http://shareware.cnet.com/

Timesheets/Project Management

1st Web timesheet remains the marketshare leader in tracking time, expenses and projects. Enterprise ready and free for 10 users or less.
www.journyx.com

Travel Brochures and Vacation Guides

Select and receive free travel brochures from America's top 100 vacation areas.. Includes state tourism guides, regions, cities, maps and more.
www.100bestvacations.com

Whale Mail

A free, easy way to send large files (up to 50 MB) without having to post them on an e-mail server.
www.whalemail.com

GENERAL INFORMATION

About.com

Lists of links and resources for just about anything, including directories for small business resources.
http://about.com

Basic Accounting

www.smartbiz.com/sbs/arts/cbf3.htm

General

Answers to your questions about just about anything—for free!
www.askjeeves.com
www.askme.com
This is an in-depth reference site. Check out the site map for an overview of all the information available here.
www.refdesk.com
General information
www.google.com
Lots of links
www.greatinfo.com
www.infoplease.com

Global Locator

Indispensable directory for business deals, phones, legal advice, yellow & white page searches, travel & shopping bargains, free games & music downloads, & educational & mapping resources.
www.geoportals.com

<u>Reference Guides</u>

Encyclopedias
www.britannica.com
www.encyclopedia.com
Microsoft's encyclopedia/dictionary/atlas
www.encarta.msn.com
The Merriam-Webster online dictionary and thesaurus.
www.m-w.com
Access to over 600 dictionaries and over 2 ½ million definitions.
www.onelook.com
Links to dictionaries in over 230 languages, grammar guides, quotations, synonyms and acronyms.
www.yourdictionary.com
Encyclopedia dedicated to computer technology
http://webopedia.internet.com/TERM/i/index.html
Reference guide about the Internet and computers.
www.whatis.com

<u>Security to Protect Your Business</u>

Communications Control Systems of New York
212-268-4779
Sheffield Electronics
312-643-4928
The Spy Store
212-366-6466

<u>Telephones</u>

Want the best telephone plan deal?
www.abelltolls.com
Free Internet answering machine. Hear incoming telephone messages in real time while surfing the Internet on the same phone line. Several programs to choose from.
www.crays.com
Audio conferencing services.
www.actionconferencecall.com

GOVERNMENT AGENCIES

Catalog of Federal Domestic Assistance
Description of Federal Domestic Assistance Programs. Information on grants, loans and more.
http://aspe.os.dhhs.gov/cfda/index.htm

Census Bureau
www.census.gov/

Equal Opportunity Employment Commission
Federal laws protect employees from age, sex and race discrimination; sexual harassment; and much more. This EEOC page for small businesses-provides the information.
www.eeoc.gov/small/index.html

Federal Trade Association
Help to avoid frauds
www.ftc.gov/bcp/menu-internet.htm

International Trade Administration
From the U.S. Department of Commerce, links, tips and details on federal help for exporters
www.ita.doc.gov/td/tic/

Small business Administration
www.sba.gov
409 Third Street SW, Washington D.C. 20416
800-827-5722

Small Business Innovative Research Program
www.darpa.mil/sbir/sbir.html

State Tax Forms
Can't find your state income tax forms? Try
www.1040.com/state.htm

Statistics
Statistics produced by 70 Federal government agencies on just about anything you can think of.
www.fedstats.gov

United States Copyright Office
www.loc.gov/copyright

United States Government Agency, Document & Resource Search Page
www.nwbuildnet.com/nwbn/govbot.html

United States Immigration and Naturalization Services
www.ins.usdoj.gov

United States Patent and Trademark Office
www.uspto.gov
2011 Crystal Drive, Arlington, VA 22202
703-305-8341
Fax 703-308-5258

U.S. Chamber of Commerce Small Business Institute
www.usccsbi.com

U.S. Securities and Exchange Commission
Is your client financially solvent? Search the EDGAR database for annual and quarterly filings submitted by established public companies.
www.sec.gov

HARDWARE/SOFTWARE/SUPPLIES

Adobe PageMill
A good software package for putting your business on the web.
www.adobe.com/products/pagemill/main.html

Clip Art
www.aplusart.com
http://webclipart.about.com/internet/web
www.nutech.com/index.html   *(especially for businesses)*

Downloads
Click on the business link for all sorts of business related software programs.
http://download.cnet.com

Front Page
Considered to be the best software for businesses.
www.microsoft.com/frontpage/

Hewett Packard
Offers technical solutions for small and home offices.
www.hp.com

Home Depot
www.homedepot.com

IBM Small Business Center
http://www-1.ibm.com/businesscenter/us/smbusapub.nsf/detailcontacts/SBCenter59BB
888-IBM-5800

OfficeMax
www.officemax.com

Pricing Manager
Software to help you get the best price for your product or service.
www.infores.com
617-890-1100

Sawtooth Technologies
Software to conduct computer-assisted surveys of any complexity.
www.sawtooth.com
847-866-0870

Trellix
Software for the cost conscious.
www.trellix.com

INSURANCE

Health Insurance
www.ehealthinsurance.com

Insurance Guide for Business Owners
www.hiaa.org/cons/guidebo.html

Life and Health Insurance Foundation for Education
www.life-line.org

INTERNATIONAL

Export Tutor
A tutorial to bring you up to speed on becoming a fast-paced exporter.
http://web.miep.org/tutor

Planet Business
A great resource for finding foreign contacts and partners
www.planetbiz.com

U.S. Trade Commission
Information regarding International Trade.
www.ita.doc.gov

LEGAL

Legal Advice for the Small Business Owner
Complete small business legal guide by Robert Friedman, Dearborn Financial Publishing. (Book $29.95)
800-533-2665

The Legal Guide for Starting and Running A Business
By Robert Steingold, Nolo Press (Software $24.95)
800-992-6656

Nolo.com
Web site devoted to legal issues.
www.nolo.com/encyclopedia/sb_ency.html

MAGAZINES AND NEWSLINKS

Amazon.com
www.Amazon.com

Big Ideas Bulletin
www.big-idea.com

Business Week
www.businessweek.com
1221 Avenue of the Americas, 39th Floor, New York, NY 10020
800-635-1200

Business 2.0
www.business2.com

Deloitte & Touche LLP Business Advisor
www.dtonline.com/ba/ba.htm

Entrepreneur.com
www.Entreprenuer.com

Entrepreneur Magazine
www.entrepreneurmag.com
Entrepreneur Media Inc., 2392 Morse Ave., Irvine CA 92614
949-261-2325

Home Business Journal
www.homebizjour.com

Inc. Magazine Online Edition
www.inc.com

IRS—The Digital Daily
www.irs.ustreas.gov/prod/cover.html

Minority Business Entrepreneur
www.mbemag.com

Money Magnet Magazine
www.anova.group.com/aisle2.html

Moneymaking Mommy
Emphasis on mothers working at home.
www.moneymakingmommy.com

NewsAlert
Comprehensive source for real-time financial and business news, stock quotes, and investment research.
www.newsalert.com

Small Biz Net
www.lowe.org/smbiznet

SmartMoney
www.SmartMoney.com

Wall Street Journal Interactive Edition
(Two weeks free)
www.wsj.com

Work At Home Success
www.workathomesuccess.com

Your Home Business Weekly
www.yourhomebizcom/enewsletter.html

MARKETING AND SALES

American Demographics Magazine
www.demographics.com

Pricemax
Applied information in Marketing
203-226-0316

Sales Magazines
www.salescreators.com
www.salesdoctors.com

Sales Marketing Network
www.info-now.com

SMALL/HOME BUSINESSES

Advanced Small Business Information
www.businesslead.com

All Freelance
Directory of freelance, contract and small business resources.
http://allfree.server101.com

American Express Small Business Exchange
www.americanexpress.com/smallbusiness

Ask The Employer
A little bit of everything, including starting your own business. Check out the eclectic links page.
www.asktheemployer.com

Business.com
Research potential clients with detailed information on over 10,000 U.S. companies.
www.business.com

Business@home
News and how-to articles to help home-based business owners adapt to the ever-changing business environment.
www.gohome.com

Business Owners Toolkit
Total know-how for small businesses.
www.toolkit.cch.com/

Home-Based Business Information
Info on multi-level marketing, marketing, franchises, etc.
www.bizoffice.com

Links to many other Small Business Sites
Small Business Directory
www.5thavenue.com/5th.html
SBA links
www.sba.gov/starting/indexoutside.html

Selling Your Business

Do you wonder how much you could get if you sold your business?
www.businessesforsale.com
www.forsale.com

Small Business Corner

www.irs.gov/bus_info/sm_bus/index.html

Small Business Know-How Resource

www.liraz.com

Small Business Knowledge Base

www.bizmove.com

Small Office

Provides B-to-B commerce services for the small and home office.
www.smalloffice.com

Working Solo

Resources for the small office home office (SOHO) crowd.
www.workingsolo.com

STAFF SEARCH

Finding Staff

Post want ads and read resumes of job seekers
www.careermosiac.com
www.careerpath.com
www.monster.com

National Salary Comparisons

U.S. wage and benefit data from the Bureau of Labor Statistics.
www.bls.gov/compub.htm

TAXES

CCH Business Owners Toolkit

Contains tax information, as well as sample business documents and financial spreadsheet templates.
www.toolkit.cch.com

Deloitte & Touche
Top-rated accounting firm can help you with your taxes.
www.dtonline.com

Federal Tax Forms
www.irs.ustreas.gov/prod/forms_pubs/forms.html

Intuit
Known for its Quicken and TurboTax software programs.
www.intuit.com

IRS Online
For small business information and online publications and forms.
www.irs.ustreas.gov/prod/bus_info/sm_bus/index.html

LA Times Online
This site offers helpful tax and business information.
www.latimes.com/taxes

MoneyNet
Breaking financial news provided by the Reuters News Agency.
www.moneynet.com/home/MONEYNET/homepage/homepage.asp

Price, Waterhouse, Coopers—Tax News Network
Another big accounting firm that can answer tax questions for you.
www.taxnews.com/tnn_public

Quicken—Small Business
Get information on taxes, borrowing money and other financial topics.
www.quicken.com/small%20business

TRAVEL

City Search
Worldwide city guide helps you find and plan what you want to do on a visit, then let's you take action such as buying event tickets or making reservations.
www.citysearch.com

Homefair Salary Calculator
Compare the cost of living in different U.S. and international cities.
www.homefair.com/homefair/cmr/salcalc.html

MapQuest
Provides maps free-of-charge.
www.mapquest.com

Traveling
www.travelocity.com

WEB RELATED

BUILDING YOUR WEB SITE

SITES TO CHECK BEFORE BUILDING YOUR WEB SITE
www.builder.com
www.webdeveloper.com
www.zdnet.com/ebusiness

How to Build Lame Web Sites
The name says it all—advice on what not to do!
http://webdevelopersjournal.co.uk/columns/perpend1.html

InterNIC
Check on availability and register domain names for your web site.
www.internic.net/

Media Metrix
Monitor your web site traffic
www.mediametrix.com

Network Solutions
The main marketplace to register U.S. domain names.
www.networksolutions.com

Net Mechanic
Check your site for bad code and broken links, free-of-charge.
www.netmechanics.com

Web Site Hosting
www.abtsonline.com
www.WebExpress.com

Top Hosts
Background material on picking a host for your web site.
www.tophosts.com

Business News
For the latest up-to-date business news
www.cnet.com

Entrepreneurs on the Web
www.entrepreneur-web.com

Free Web Site and Tips
FreeWebspace.net is a searchable index of more than 250 different free web hosts. Free web space for your personal or business site.
www.freewebspace.net
Free tips, links and resource to increase your traffic and generate $ using your Web site.
www.wealthjet.com
Highly successful Internet marketers spill the beans at a new private Web site. Click now for instant access and watch your online profits soar, guaranteed! Free subscription via e-mail.
www.marketingchallenge.com

Interactive Guide to the Internet
www.sierramm.com/smpnet.html

Internet Statistics
This site links to all sorts of statistical data.
www.internetstats.com

Major Online Providers
America Online (AOL)
www.aol.com
800-827-6364

CompuServ
www.compuserv.com
800-848-8199

Earthlink
www.earthlink.com
888-327-8454

Genie
www.genie.com
800-638-9636

Geocities
http://geocities.yahoo.com/

Microsoft Network (MSN)
www.msn.com
800-386-5550

Prodigy
www.prodigy.com
800-776-3449

Net Ratings
Web sites ranked by traffic volume
www.netratings.com

Phone Numbers
The Internet 800/888 Directory
http://inter800.com.search.htm
Search for phone numbers and e-mail addresses
www.switchboard.com
www.tollfree.att.net/tf.html
The Ultimate Yellow Pages
www.theultimates.com/yellow/
List of all area codes
www.nanpa.com

Radio Stations
www.broadcast.com

Success
If you'd like to hear many of America's most successful people like: **Tony Robbins, Brian Tracy, Jack LaLanne, Ed McMahon, Tom Hopkins, Paul Harvey or Jimmy Connors** *talk about their Entrepreneurial success—listen to my radio show,* **Entrepreneur Spotlight** *live on the web every Wednesday, 1—2 pm E.S.T. Check it out on*
www.wpon.com

SOHO Radio
Internet's only radio network by and for today's small/home office worker.
www.sohoradio.com

Robots on the Web
Referred to as Bots, these cyberrobots can perform a variety of missions for you by searching dozens of sites at one time.

www.biddersedge.com	*(searches auctions)*
www.vsn.net/af	*(searches auctions)*
http://botspot.com/search/s-shop.htm	*(listing of other bots)*
www.bottomdollar.com	*(all purpose shopping)*
www.mysimon.com	*(shopping)*

Search Engines

www.alltheweb.com	
www.altavista.com	
www.b2bscene.com	*(for business related searches)*
http://botspot.com/search/s-shop.htm	*(Bots by category)*
www.dogpile.com	
www.excite.com	
www.fastsearch.com	
www.go.com	
www.highway61.com	
www.itools.com/find-it/	
www.lycos.com	
www.netsearcher.com	
www.snap.com	
www.yahoo.com	

Web Assured
E-tailer evaluater
www.webassured.com

Wireless Web
Hoiley
Free tool for creating wireless application protocol complaint sites.
www.hoiley.com

Tag Tag
Free tool to help you make your web site wireless web-ready.
www.inetis.com/english/solutions_tagtag.htm

WAPLY
Directory of wireless web sites.
www.waply.com

THE ULTIMATE ENTREPRENEUR RESOURCE

www.PatrickGilligan.com